FIRST AMERICAN

CATHOLIC PILGRIMAGE

TO

PALESTINE, 1889.

BY
REV. JAMES PFEIFFER.

Published by Left of Brain Books

Copyright © 2021 Left of Brain Books

ISBN 978-1-396-32170-2

First Edition

All rights reserved. No part of this publication may be reproduced, distributed, or transmitted in any form or by any means, including photocopying, recording, or other electronic or mechanical methods, without the prior written permission of the publisher, except in the case of brief quotations embodied in critical reviews and certain other noncommercial uses permitted by copyright law. Left of Brain Books is a division of Left of Brain Onboarding Pty Ltd.

DEDICATED
TO
OUR PILGRIMS.

Table of Contents

Preface.	1
On Leaving New York.	3
List Of Members.	4
Cherbourg.	9
Paris.	10
Marseilles.	11
Nice.	13
Genoa.	13
Pisa.	14
Florence.	15
Assisi.	16
Rome.	19
Monte Casino.	28
Naples.	28
Alexandria.	32
Cairo.	36
Ismailia.	44
The Suez Canal.	45
Port Said.	45
Jaffa.	46
Lydda.	49
Ramleh.	49
Latroum.	51
History of Jerusalem.	53
Trip from Jerusalem to Jericho.	73
Dead Sea.	76
The Jordan.	76
The Quarantine Mountain.	77
Bethania.	78
Bethlehem.	79
Few Remarks about the Present Jerusalem.	81
Our Certificate of Jerusalem.	83
Bethel.	83
Naplous.	85
Nazareth.	88
Mount Thabor.	90

THE LAKE OF GENESARETH OR TIBERIAS.	91
CANA OF GALILEE.	93
MOUNT CARMEL.	93
ST. JOHN D'ACRE.	95
BEYROUT.	95
THE ISLAND OF CYPRUS.	96
SMYRNA.	96
EPHESUS.	97
SMYRNA.—CONTINUED.	98
THE DARDANELLES.	99
THE SEA OF MARMORA.	100
CONSTANTINOPLE.	100
THE BOSPORUS.	107
ATHENS, GREECE.	107
THE COSTUMES OF GREECE.	114
THE GULF OF CORINTH, OR LEPANTO.	115
BRINDISI.	117
LORETO.	117
VENICE.	118
MILAN.	120
ST. GOTHARD'S TUNNEL, SWITZERLAND.	122
LAKE OF THE FOUR FOREST CANTONS.	123
LUCERNE.	124
MOUNT RIGI.	125
MARIA EINSIEDELN.	126
BASEL.	127
STRASBURG.	128
SPEYER.	129
MUNICH.	130
NUREMBERG.	132
WUERZBURG.	133
FRANKFORT-ON-THE-MAIN.	134
MENTZ (GER. MAINZ.)	134
THE RHINE.	135
COLOGNE.	136
HAMBURG.	137

PREFACE.

SINCE the First American Catholic Pilgrimage to Palestine was so grand, memorable, and ever blissful, and, as the title says, the first one of this great Country of ours, since the 400 years of its discovery, I time and again thought to myself that its history ought to be written, and therefore, since none, more able than myself, have done so, I hereby, dear reader, will give you its history. For a christian and more so, a catholic, the dangerous journey to the Holy Land is the most interesting of all travels. There the learned find a large field for their researches, whilst the pious christian can scarcely move a step without meeting a sanctuary, or a monument familiar to him by name, but venerated from a great distance only. Words are not adequate, much less am I able to express the sweet emotions, the holy raptures of the christian soul when, in presence of the places where he reads the short but comprehensive words: "Here is the spot where stood the manger in which was laid the Infant Son of God;" or, "Here the Word was made Flesh." Who does not burst out in tears of joy, when pressing his lips on the sacred stone of the Holy Sepulchre; who can remain unmoved at the sight of Calvary, whereon took place the final scene of that awful drama, and what thoughts of regeneration do not refresh our minds, when we drink of Jordan's waters, when following the footsteps of Jesus along the shores of the beautiful Lake of Tiberias, or when taking a boat-ride on it with Christ as it were. What genuine sensations does the traveler not experience when he is winding his way along the zigzag path of the lovely Thabor, or visiting so many other places, sanctified by the presence, and illustrated by so many miracles of our Saviour.

These Holy Places, which are dear to every true christian, are still under the sway of Mohammedans, Turks, Schismatics Greeks, Armenians and Copts. If we would more fully realize this deplorable condition we would and ought to contribute more to the collection for the rescue of the Holy Places, which is ordered by our Rt. Rev. Bishops on Good Friday. It is this principally, that induced me to write this book. That Almighty God may move the minds and hearts of the reader, is the sincere wish of

THE AUTHOR.

ON LEAVING NEW YORK.

AT about 9 o'clock A. M. on the 20th of February, the day previous our leaving New York city, the pilgrims all assembled at the beautiful residence of the Commissary of the Holy Land for the United States, the VERY REV. CHAS. A. VISSANI, O. S. F.

Here each pilgrim received a silver medal, which was struck for the occasion, the obverse representing the Crucifixion on Calvary, with the inscription, "*First American Pilgrimage to the Holy Land*, 1889," while the reverse is decorated with the SACRED HEARTS OF JESUS AND MARY, and the name of the pilgrim. On our reaching Jerusalem these medals were blessed on the Holy Sepulchre, and are now to each one a precious memento.

A beautiful banner was furthermore procured by the VERY REV. CHAS. A. VISSANI, which the pilgrims, on their reaching Jerusalem, deposited at the Holy Sepulchre. Said banner has on the one side the figure of our Lord rising from the Sepulchre, with the words of Isaias, "*And His Sepulchre shall be Glorious*"; on the other the American coat of arms and the inscription, "*First American Pilgrimage to the Holy Land*, 1889."

After each one had his medal, the banner was blessed and a procession was formed, headed by the banner carried by Father VISSANI, and the pilgrims thus marched to the grand cathedral, (said to be the finest church in America and to have cost three millions of dollars,) where the RT. REV. W. M. WIGGER, D. D., bishop of Newark, N. J., celebrated Mass, that the pilgrims might have a happy journey. Present in the sanctuary were: MT. REV. MICHAEL A.

CORRIGAN, D.D., archbishop of New York, and RT. REV. JOSEPH RADEMACHER, D. D., bishop of Nashville, Tenn. As the sacrifice of Mass was over, the MOST REV. MICHAEL A. CORRIGAN ascended the pulpit and preached a very eloquent and appropriate sermon, his text being: "*Here I stood.*"

In the afternoon those pilgrims, who had no passports, had them procured by Messrs. Cook & Son, the world-renowned tourists, who, with Father Vissani, organized and conducted the pilgrimage. The pilgrims purchased their roundtrip tickets from Thos. Cook & Son, New York. For their surplus money they received letters of credit from Cook & Son, which were payable in all countries and at every point of the route, in the currency of the various countries through which the pilgrims passed. The usual allowance of 200 lbs. of baggage was made by the Steamship Companies, in Europe and in the East 60 lbs. were allowed each adult passenger. The next day, the 21st of February, at 10 o'clock A. M., the following pilgrims went on board of the steamer "Wieland" of the Hamburg-American Steamer Line, at Hoboken, N. J., and sailed for Cherbourg, (France):

LIST OF MEMBERS.

FIRST SECTION.

Rev. Anthony Arnold,	Brooklyn, N. Y.
Rev. Wendelin Guhl,	" "
Rev. Adam F. Tonner,	New York City.
Rev. P. M. Kennedy,	Birmingham, Conn.
Rev. John Russell,	New Haven, Conn.
Rev. A. G. Spierings,	Keyport, N. J.
Rev. A. Hurly,	Rosemount, Minn.
Rev. J. J. Gabriel,	St. Leon, Ind.
Mr. Jacob Shandorf,	Manlius Station, N.Y.
Mr. Patrick Lilly,	New York City.
Mrs. C. P. Lilly,	" "
Mr. John B. Manning,	" "

Master Robert Collier,	" "
Mr. J. T. Michan,	" "
Mrs. J. T. Michan,	" "
Mr. Michael W. Costello,	Boston, Mass.
Mr. John P. Brady,	Baltimore, Md.
Mr. T. H. Bowes,	Columbus, O.
Mr. Jos. Donahue,	Columbus, Miss.
Miss Mary McFarland,	Boston, Mass.
Miss Bridget Kilkenny,	" "
Miss Annie Weaver,	Brooklyn, N. Y.
Miss E. A. Ford,	New York City.
Miss Fannie Herle,	Boston, Mass.
Miss Mary Connelly,	" "
Miss Julia Harrington,	Charlestown, Mass.
Miss Annie Doherty,	" "
Miss A. E. F. Brewer,	Philadelphia, Pa.
Miss F. G. Snyder,	" "
Miss E. McCarthy,	Denver, Col.
Miss Helen Dannemille,	Canton, O.
Miss Mary F. Deveny,	Boston, Mass.

SECOND SECTION.

Rev. F. Bender,	Pueblo, Col.
Rev. Lucas Gottbehoede, O. S. F.,	Cincinnati, O.
Rev. J. T. Durward,	Baraboo, Wis.
Rev. J. J. Dunn,	Meadville, Pa.
Rev. J. Buckley,	Beaver Dam, Wis.
Mr. Jas. Lee,	Plymouth, Pa
Mr. Theodore Mottu,	Baltimore, Md.
Mr. Jas. C. Connor,	Chicago, Ill.
Mr. Frank Headen,	" "
Mr. Daniel McCann,	" "
Mr. Wm. P. Ginther,	Akron, O.
Mr. Wm. Byrne,	Jacksonville, Fla.

Mrs. Wm. Byrne,	" "
Mrs. Jane Nolan,	
Miss Alice Byrne,	
Miss Mary Jane Byrne	" "
Miss S. L. Burke,	Philadelphia, Pa.

Third Section.

Rt. Rev. W. M. Wigger, D. D., Bishop of Newark, N. J.
Rt. Rev. Joseph Rademacher. D. D., Bishop of Nashville, Tenn.

Rt. Rev. Monsignor Seton,	Jersey City, N. J.
Very Rev. Chas. A. Vissani,	New York City.
Very Rev. John F. Fierens, V. G.,	Portland, Ore.
Rev. M. J. Phelan,	New York City.
Rev. James Pfeiffer,	Enochsburg, Ind.
Rev. John Walsh,	Troy, N. Y.
Rev. J. M. Nardiello,	Bloomfield, N. J.
Rev. Frederick Kivelitz,	Freehold, N. J.
Rev. L. C. Carroll,	Jersey City, N. J
Rev. W. P. Cantwell,	Metuchen, N. J.
Rev. J. C. Dunn,	Newark, N. J.
Rev. J. A. O'Grady,	New Brunswick, N. J.
Rev. M. E. Kane,	Red Bank, N. J.
Rev. M. Carroll,	Allegheny City, Penn.
Rev. Geo. Meyer,	Fryburg, Pa.
Rev. Christopher Hughes,	Fall River, Mass.
Rev. P. J. Harkins,	Holyoke, Mass.
Rev. J. J. Keogh,	Milwaukee, Wis.
Rev. Stephen Traut,	Racine, Wis.
Very Rev. H. Robinson, V. G.,	Leadville, Col.
Rev. H. J. Rousseau,	Ispheming, Mich.
Rev. F. J. Blanc,	Pass Christian, Miss.
Rev. John Harty,	Providence, R. I.

Rev. John Koeberle,	Brooklyn, N. Y.
Mr. Jas. T. Quinn,	Albany, N. Y.
Mr. James C. Farrell,	" "
Mr. A. Neupert,	Buffalo, N Y.
Mr. Chas. Bork,	" "
Mr. John Ford,	New York City.
Mr. J. Herbert Ledwith,	" "
Mr. Alois Muller,	" "
Mr. Joseph F. Ismay,	" "
Mr. Wm. Noonan,	Elizabethport, N. J.
Mrs. M. Noonan,	" "
Mr. C. P. Harkins,	Newton, Mass.
Mr. Patrick Coyle,	Waterbury, Conn.
Mr. Jos. Lefebre,	St. Paul, Minn.
Mr. Louis Dion,	" "
Mr. John H. Hoebing,	Wall Lake, Iowa.
Dr. Wm. E. Carroll,	Jersey City, N. J
Miss Elizabeth C. McCartin,	" "
Miss Isabel T. McCartin,	" "
Miss Katie Daly,	" "
Miss C. Quinn,	Albany, N.Y.
Miss Carrie Cantwell,	Fall River, Mass.
Miss Catherine Harkings,	Holyoke, Mass.
Miss Grace M. Harkins,	" "
Miss Annie Carroll,	Allegheny City, Pa.
Miss Josephine J. McCall,	New York City.
Miss Marie F. Farnham,	" "

The pilgrims were divided, as you will perceive from the above, into three sections, that is to say, all left New York on the same steamer with the intention to remain together until they had reached and viewed Jerusalem and the important points surrounding it.

On the journey to Jerusalem we first visited Paris, then Marseilles, Nice, Genoa, Pisa, Florence, Assisi, Rome, Naples, Alexandria, Cairo, the Pyramids,

Ismailia, the Suez Canal, Port-Said, Jaffa, Jerusalem, Bethlehem, the Dead Sea, the river Jordan and Jericho.

After this the first section left for New York via Jaffa, Alexandria, Genoa, Turin, Mount Cenis Tunnel, Paris and Havre, an attractive trip of eighty-four days. A very good and praiseworthy arrangement Cook & Son made with the pilgrims—any one of either section could branch off and leave the party at any time; some actually did so, Cook & Son refunding the money *pro rata*.

The price of this section, including all necessary expenses, first-class on steamers and at hotels, and second-class by rail, was $460.00; first-class across the Atlantic and second-class beydon was $425.00.

The second section included all the places of the first section, as stated above, and the long tour in Palestine, viz.: Samaria, Nazareth, Lake of Galilee, Mount Carmel, Tyre, Sidon, and Beyrout, a 98 days' trip, price including all necessary expenses: first-class on steamers and at hotels, and second-class by rail, $530.00; first-class across the Atlantic, and second-class beyond, $490.00. Beyrout was the terminus of the second section, having the same itinerary home as the first section.

The third section included all the places of the first section, the long tour in Palestine (from Jerusalem to Beyrout, via Samaria, Galilee and Tyre), Smyrna and Ephesus, Constantinople, Athens, Corinth, Brindisi, Venice, Milan, St. Gotthart Tunnel and Lucerne, a most magnificent trip of 112 days, price including all necessary expenses: first-class on steamers and at hotels, and second-class by rail, $650.00; first-class across the Atlantic and second-class beyond, $600.00.

Now we are ready to sail from New York.

As the steamer was loaded and every thing ready, it majestically left the shores of the United States, and moved on, out into the great Atlantic ocean, while hundreds of friends, who had escorted the pilgrims to the shore, waved their handkerchiefs, shouted, and wished us all a happy journey and safe return. The first two days the weather was most beautiful, the ocean calm, and the pilgrims were all in very good humor, so much so, that on the second evening, the 22d of February, the pilgrims gave a kind of a concert for the stewards, it being the birthday of the *Father of our Liberty*. On this occasion, Rt. Rev. Bishop Wigger, Rt. Rev. Bishop Rademacher, and Monsignor Seton made appropriate speeches.

On the third day, however, a fearful storm arose, which lasted uninterruptedly for six or seven days, in consequence of which all the pilgrims, excepting Monsignor Seton, experienced, *nolens volens,* what seasickness is. The Atlantic ocean is that branch of the general ocean, which separates the continents of Europe and Africa from America. It is named the Atlantic Ocean from Mount Atlas, which rises near its shores. It is supposed by some professional men, such as Dr. Young, to have a depth of about 15,000 ft. The distance or length from New York to France is about three thousand miles. To be on this immense ocean in time of a storm is no fun. The storm ceased about two days before we landed, and when the ocean became somewhat tranquil I amongst other priests said Mass on the steamer, we having a portable altar with us. As soon as the storm was over, the seasickness also left us, and the good humor of the pilgrims revived. The last evening we were on the Atlantic the pilgrims gave a second concert in honor of the captain, who, at the conclusion thereof, expressed his thanks, and enjoyed us with the announcement, that if we would go on deck we could see European light, whereupon we rushed on deck and were agreeably surprised to behold a European light-house. As we were obliged to pass through the English Channel for quite a distance, we did not land until about 5 o'clock the next evening.

On the last day we spent on the steamer, which happened to be on a Sunday, Rt. Rev. Bishop Wigger read the Gospel of the day and delivered a sermon to the pilgrims, with the following text: *"Behold, we go up to Jerusalem,"* (St, Luke, chap. XVIII, v. 31,) which was contained in the day's gospel. The Rt. Rev. Bishop in his eloquent and touching sermon, together with other truths, proved to us, that these words applied in an especial manner to us happy American Pilgrims.

Being thus again encouraged and strenghtened we landed safely at

CHERBOURG.

At 5 o'clock in the evening of the 2d day of March. As soon as we came ashore our valises were searched by custom-house officers. It seems the French like tobacco, because that was the principal thing they looked for. After that we went to our hotel, which was shown us by Cook's guides, who had come to meet and guide the pilgrims on their entire journey. After supper we all had to go to the custom-house proper, to have our trunks searched. In the evening some of the pilgrims went to a church, in which at the time 40 hours devotion was held. Right Rev. Bishop Rademacher had the honor to give benediction with the Blessed Sacrament at the close of the evening's devotion.

The next morning, at about 6 o'clock, we took the train to Paris. The distance from Cherbourg to Paris is about 200 miles.

Heating Cars in France.

The first thing on the train to Paris, amongst other things that excited our admiration, was the peculiar way the French heat the cars. Before the train leaves the depot they shove tin cans, of about 5 ft. long, 8 in. wide and about 5 in. high, which are filled with hot water, under the feet of the passengers. When this water has become cold, after having traveled a distance of about 50 miles and they stop at a depot, the cans are taken out and others, also filled with hot water, take their places.

When the train moves on again the doors of the cars are locked until they come to a stopping place. Much could here be said about the construction of the cars. The pilgrims had nothing to do with buying tickets or looking after their baggage, as the guide looked after all this, making it very convenient for us.

At 7 o'clock in the evening of March 3d we reached Paris. Here in the depot, as in every other large city, our guides gave each one a ticket showing the name of the hacks—which were standing ready for us at the depot—and also the name of our hotel, and when all of us had entered the hacks, we were driven to the GRAND HOTEL.

PARIS.

Paris, the capital of France, and the second city in Europe in point of population, is on the banks of the river Seine and has a population of about 3,852,000. Paris is noted, amongst other things, for its beautiful churches and its architecture. The New Opera House is said to be the finest in the world. Amongst the churches the most impressive of all is the cathedral of *Notre Dame*, a noble specimen of the early pointed style of so-called Gothic; it is cruciform, with an extreme length of 390 ft., width of transepts 144 ft., height of vaulting 105 ft., width of western front 128 ft., flanked by two massive towers 224 ft. high.[1] Its immense Thesaurus was also shown to us.

THE GRAND OPERA OF PARIS.

The largest and finest theatre in the world is the New Grand Opera of Paris. It was begun in 1860 and opened to the public for the first time on January 5th, 1875. It was built at the expense of the government, and cost $5,600,000, exclusive of the land which it occupies. Notwithstanding the vast size of the building, the auditorium contains only 2,194 seats. By far the greater part of the building is occupied by a vast number of rooms, halls, staircases, shops, etc., appurtenances designed for the convenience and pleasure of the spectators and of those connected with the theatre. The stage is about 100 ft. in width by 220 ft. in depth, and 700 singers can be grouped upon it. In its facilities for ingress and egress, in the completeness of its machinery and appliances, and in the magnificence and costliness of its decorations it far surpasses any theatre of modern times. (Thus Appleton's Cyclopædia has it.) "France is the centre of civilized nations, Paris is the centre of France, the 'Boulevards des Italiens' is the centre of Paris," says an enthusiastic modern Parisian. In the Church of St. Louis forming a part of the Invalides, we also saw the tomb of Napoleon I., the great porphyry sarcophagus standing directly under the dome which crowns the edifice.

MARSEILLES.

We left Paris March the 4th, in the evening, and traveled by day express train to Marseilles, the distance being about 400 miles, and arrived at 7 o'clock P. M. on March 5th.

---

[1] Appleton's Cyclopædia.

On our way from Paris to Marseilles we came through Lyons, which is especially noted for its silk factories. We also came through Avignon, called the Babilonian exile of the popes. Here all the popes, from Clement V. to Gregory XI. (1309—77) made their residence. The pilgrims saw the palace in which the popes lived. The last named pope restored the Papal See to Rome. The 14th century was thus the period of the city's greatest splendor. It then numbered about 100,000 inhabitants.

Marseilles is the principal seaport of France. All parts of the city are well supplied with water through a canal fed by the Durance, and opened in 1850, at a cost of $10,000,000. The public buildings possess little architectural interest. The cathedral is said to have been built upon the site of a temple of Diana; the Church of St. Victor is the most ancient church, and was formerly one of the most celebrated abbeys in Christendom. In it the pilgrims saw the confessional, altar, chapel and tomb of St. Lazarus, its first bishop, whom Christ resuscitated. St. Lazarus lived in this grotto, with St. Mary Magdalena who here led a contemplative life; whilst Martha was of a busy character and built a convent at Avignon. After the ascension of Christ the Jews persecuted Lazarus, Mary Magdalena and Martha, put them in a ship without sails, thinking they would thus perish, but they all three landed at Marseilles. Here we also saw the cross, on which St. Andrew the Apostle was crucified. The pilgrims here in Marseilles, furthermore visited the renowned church "*Notre Dame de la Garde*," the sailors' shrine, 700 feet above the level of the sea. This church has the following history: At one time, sailors on the Mediterranean Sea, near Marseilles, were in great danger of being shipwrecked, and they made a promise to the Blessed Virgin, whom the Church designates, "the Star of the Ocean," that they would build a church in her honor if they were saved, whereupon, in the evening, the sailors saw a star on the top of the hill, where now this church stands, built by these sailors. The walls of this church are bedecked with offerings and above the High Altar appear the words: "Ave Maris Stella." It is generally visited by Catholics for thanksgiving after having crossed the ocean. In one of the streets of Marseilles is also a statue of the Immaculate Conception B. V. M., thirty feet high, with this inscription: "Raised by the archbishop, priests and people of Marseilles, on the 8th of December, 1857, to perpetuate the decree of the Immaculate Conception, by Pope Pius IX."

NICE.

On March the 6th, the pilgrims took the train for Nice. We arrived at four o'clock in the evening, and stopped at the Grand Hotel, which has six hundred bed rooms, and is the finest hotel we saw on our trip. The distance from Marseilles to Nice is two hundred miles. Nice which numbers a population of 80,000, is a seaport, and the larger part of it was ceded to France by Italy in 1860. It has narrow streets, but from its centre rises a hill eight hundred feet high. The summit, upon which formerly a castle had been built, is now laid out in public pleasure grounds. It is inhabited chiefly by English, who have a chapel and two cemeteries. The houses are very neat and encompassed by beautiful gardens.

The town contains a cathedral of the seventeenth century, a national college, a public library hospitals, convents, a zoological museum, a theatre and baths. Nice is a free port, and steamers run three times a week to Marseilles and Genoa. It is chiefly noted as a watering place and a resort for English invalids, who frequent it in such numbers, that they have produced a complete change in the aspect of that part of town which they inhabit. As many as 5,000 or 6,000 British visitors are found here in the winter. The climate is remarkably mild and solubrious, and the suburbs, which lie among the low hills a mile or two inland, are particularly delightful.

March the 7th, we took the evening train for

GENOA.

After we had left Genoa, we came to Ventimille, which is on the boundary line of France and Italy. Here we had to go through another custom-house. We thought the custom-house officials at Cherbourg were strict, but we found them here (in Italy) more severe; they were regular robbers. We had a terrible time of it. One of our priests had with him about fifty cigars. As soon as they noticed that, two or three policemen held him, took the cigars and kept them. The priest being an American, was of course out-spoken, and called them "*Latros*," i. e. thieves, as an officer came and tapped him on the shoulder. Some of our parties told the priest to hold his peace, or he might get into trouble. Another priest, a rather old and nice gentleman, had with him about thirty cigars and a little snuff. They confiscated all of this and fined him fifty franks—about ten dollars to our American money. I must say, that for myself I fared much better. As soon as they brought my trunk into the custom-house, I opened it, and there being no one to see me, took out my cigars (about thirty), put them in my overcoat, closed the trunk and then called an officer to look into my trunk. He did so, found everything in order, closed the trunk and put a mark on it with his chalk; a sign that it had passed the custom-house, and done I was.

We arrived at Genoa, at ten o'clock in the evening. Here we had the worst hotel on our whole trip; it would have been fit for those custom-house officials. The next morning we here visited the Cathedral, Church of the Annunziata, Palace of the Doges, Public Gardens and Cemetery, said to be the finest in the world. At the depot we also saw a monument of Christopher Columbus, this city being the place of his birth. The pilgrims also saw the body of St. Catherine. The distance from Nice to Genoa is one hundred miles.

In the evening of March the 8th, we took the train to

PISA.

In traveling from Genoa to Pisa, the train skirts the shore of the blue Mediterranean Sea, affording magnificent views as the train passes from one tunnel to another in rapid succession, there being fifty-six of these between Genoa and Pisa. From Genoa to Pisa the distance is 118 miles.

Pisa has a population of 265,959, the principal river being the Arno. It is built on a plain and is surrounded by an ancient wall with fire gates and protected by a citadel.

The cathedral, baptistry, leaning tower and Campo Sancto of Pisa, are four of the most remarkable structures in the world. They are all built of white marble and of corresponding style. The pilgrims visited these four structures.

The cathedral, finished early in the seventeenth century, contains some celebrated works of art. Its bronze doors are opened by machinery; forty men could not open them. Two of its columns are over eight hundred years old. One of its altars is solid silver; it has forty altars and three pulpits.

The baptistry, finished later than the cathedral, is a circular edifice, 160 feet in diameter and 179 feet high, with mosaic pavement and carved columns. It has 150 statues placed around its cornices.² It has a most beautiful pulpit, which Napoleon I. tried to take to Paris, but, as he had not sufficient time, he destroyed many figures on it. The columns that support it, are taken from the different Islands of the Mediterranean Sea, and, if a person sings in it, it sounds like a grand pipe organ.

The Leaning Tower of Pisa, the only leaning tower in the world, was begun in 1174 by Bonanus of Pisa and William of Innspruck. It is 179 feet high, cylindrical in form, and 50 feet in diameter; the walls on the summit are eight feet thick. The summit, on which I stood, is reached by 330 steps, that lead up in the inside. The fact which gives it the name, by which it is so well known, is, that it leans about thirteen feet from the perpendicular. This fault was manifested before its completion, and was guarded against by extra braces, and an adaptation of the stone in the highest portion. The seven bells on the top, the largest of which weighs 12,000 pounds, are so placed as to counteract by their gravity the leaning of the tower.

The *Campo Sancto*, the cemetery of Pisa, is a beautiful oblong court, 490 feet long and 170 feet wide, surrounded by arcades of white marble, 60 feet high and adorned with ancient Etruscan, Greek and Roman bass-reliefs and other sculptures, and with paintings by the early Italian masters. In its centre is an enormous mound of earth, said to have been brought from Mount Calvary, during the crusades, and formerly used as a burial ground.³ This cemetery is the pantheon of the Pisans, and among its most famous monuments is the tomb of Algarotti, erected by Frederick the Great in 1764.

March 9th we took the evening train for

FLORENCE.

We arrived at Florence at eight o'clock in the evening. It is fifty miles from Pisa to Florence, which has a population of 200,000. The city lies in a beautiful, well wooded, and cultivated valleys, surrounded by the Apennines. The river Arno flows through the city, the larger part of it being on the right or north

---

² Appleton's Cyclopædia.
³ Appleton's Cyclopædia.

bank. The river within the city is crossed by four fine stone bridges, of which the most noted is the "Ponte di Santa Trinita." It is adorned with statues, is 323 feet long and the central arch has a span of 96 feet. The "Ponte Vecchio" is 75 feet wide, and the carriage-way in the middle is lined on each side by a row of shops, occupied chiefly by goldsmiths and jewelers.

Florence has 172 churches. The "Duomo," or "Cathedral Church of Santa Maria del Fiore," which the pilgrims among others visited, is a vast and superb structure, which is surpassed in architectural grandeur only by St. Peter's in Rome. The length of the church is nearly 500 feet and of the united transepts 306 feet; its height, from the pavement to the summit of the cross, is 387 feet; the height of the nave is 153 feet, and of the side aisles, 96 feet; and, the width of the nave and aisles is 128 feet. The exterior of the church is covered throughout with red, white and black marble, disposed in panels and variagated figures. The pavement also is of many-colored marble, much of which was laid under the direction of Michael Angelo. The dome of this cathedral is the largest in the world, its circumference being greater than that of the dome of St. Peter. It excited the admiration of Michael Angelo, to whom it served as a model for the dome of St. Peter.

Near the Cathedral stands the Campanile or Belfry, which was begun in 1334. It is a square tower, 276 feet high, light and elegant, Gothic style, and divided into four lofty stories. Charles V. used to say that it deserves to be kept in a glass case.[4]

The pilgrims furthermore visited the famous galleries, such as: the Uffizi and the "Pitti Palace," which contain a collection of the choicest gems of art extant; also the Tombs of the Medicis, and the Baptistry, with its marvelous bronze doors. The pilgrims left Florence on the 13th of March and took the morning train for Assisi.

ASSISI.

The pilgrims arrived at four o'clock in the evening of the same day. From Florence to Assisi is one hundred miles. It is picturesquely situated on a

---

[4] Appleton's Cyclopædia.

declivity of a steep hill, and has a population of 5,000. It is especially noted as the birthplace of St. Francis, the founder of the Order of Franciscans. Monsignor Staniero, from Rome, came to meet the pilgrims. Here are the church and monastery in which St. Francis is buried. As soon as we arrived at the station, we took carriages, and drove up the hill about two miles, to the town proper of Assisi.

On arriving at the church in which St. Francis is buried, we were received most friendly by the Franciscan fathers, who immediately showed us the church. The church has three naves, one of which the Italian government secularized. At the time we were visiting the church, some men were at work frescoing it for a museum.

While here at Assisi we saw many things of great interest to us all. First of all the coffin that contains the body of St. Francis, the sheet in which he died, the board on which his body was washed after death, the linen with which St. Clara washed the wounds of St. Francis, the cingulum of St. Francis, in which he received the stigmata, and above all, the Veil of the Blessed Virgin Mary, said to have been brought here by the crusaders.

We then went to the Church of St. Clara; here we saw the stable in which St. Francis was born, the miraculous cross, that spoke to him whilst in prayer, the house in which St. Clara lived; we went into the chapel in which St. Clara said her divine office with her Nuns, the chair on which she sat, saw and heard the bell ring with which St. Clara called her Nuns to prayer, the breviary out of which she said her divine office, and finally saw her body.

After we had seen all this, the pilgrims were shown to hotels. I lodged in the Monastery of the Portiuncula, which is near the rail-road station, two miles from the city of Assisi, on a beautiful plain. This large and beautiful church, built over the Portiuncula chapel, has thirty-six altars. I said Mass in this portiuncula chapel the next morning. I shall here give the reader a short history of

THE PORTIUNCULA INDULGENCE.

Whilst one night St. Francis was praying in solitude, it was revealed to him, that Christ and his blessed Mother with a host of heavenly spirits, is awaiting him in the old chapel. St. Francis joyfully went there at once. As he beheld

Jesus and his mother he fell upon his knees in adoration. Christ then said to his servant: "Francis, demand what thou wilt for the salvation of souls, for thou hast been given to the world as a light, and to the terrestrial Church as a support." Upon this Francis answered: "Most holy Father and highest Lord, although I am a poor and miserable sinner, nevertheless I venture for the sake of mankind, the following grace: Grant everyone, that visits this Church, forgiveness of all his sins and punishment, after he has confessed them to a priest and obtained absolution. I pray to the blessed Virgin, our advocate, to support my petition." The Queen of heaven immediately heard his prayer and asked her divine Son to grant the petition of Francis. Hereupon the Lord answered: "Francis, what thou askest is a great deal, nevertheless thou deservest to be favored still more. I will grant thy petition, but go to my representative, Pope Honorius III, who is at Perugia, (Perugia is 13 miles, E. S. E. from Assisi,) and ask of him the desired Indulgence."

The next morning Francis went to Perugia. As he was admitted to the Pope, he said, in his great simplicity of heart: "Holy Father, some time ago I improved a Church in honor of the Mother of God. I entreat your Holiness to annex with this an Indulgence without obligation of an offering." The Pope answered: "It is not becoming to grant such favors; whoever wishes to gain an Indulgence must perform some good works. And for how many years do you ask such indulgence; for one or three years? Or, do you want me to grant it for six or seven years? With this St. Francis was not satisfied. "Oh, gracious Lord and Pope," he answered, "that is not worth while." "What shall I do then for you?" "On account of the many favors the Lord has bestowed upon this place," St. Francis answered, "with the sanction of your Holiness, I wish that all those, who visit this Church, after having confessed their sins and received absolution, may obtain remission of all their guilt in heaven and on earth, for all sins they may have committed since their baptism. I furthermore wish that they should have no other obligation to fulfill." "Francis," the Pope said, "you ask something very great; the Roman Curie is not in the habit of granting such an Indulgence." Francis answered with animosity: "Your Holiness, I do not ask it in my name, but in the name of Christ, who sends me to you." In this holy name the Pope answered: "So then be it granted" and added,: "I want it, you shall have it! you shall have it! you shall have it! Be it done in the name of the Lord."

St. Francis left Perugia on the same day, and during the night heard a voice from heaven: "Francis, know you, that the Indulgence which has been granted thee on earth, is ratified in heaven."

This Indulgence can be gained on the first Sunday in August, by all who fulfill the above named conditions in a Franciscan Church.

On March the 14th the pilgrims took the afternoon train for

ROME.

From Assisi to Rome the distance is 125 miles. It numbers 400,000 inhabitants. We arrived here March 15th, at three o'clock in the afternoon, and remained until the 25th. As we were yet eleven miles from the eternal city, we already saw the Dome of St. Peter.

The first day the pilgrims immediately went first of all, to see the grandest Church on earth, *St. Peter's*, said to be worth at present $150,000,000. A flight of twenty-seven large marble steps lead up into the grand Basilica. Of this Church, Michael Angelo said: "I will hang the Pantheon in the air in St. Peter's Dome." It holds 52,000 people. Pre-eminent among the Christian temples of the world is St. Peter's Church, the work of many Popes and architects, finally consecrated by Pope Urban VIII. in 1626, which Gibbon calls, "the most glorious structure that has ever been applied to the use of religion." The basilica of St. Peter's is surpassed by no cathedral in antiquity and splendor, and equalled by none in magnitude. Pope Sixtus V. gave 100,000 gold crowns annually towards the completion of its present Dome, finished in 1590, by Giacomo della Porta. The Church was dedicated by Pope Urban VIII. (1614) on November 18th, 1626.

The building of St. Peter's, from its foundation in 1450, till its dedication, took 175 years; and if we include the work done under Pius VI, three and a half centuries passed, before it was completed, during which time forty-three Popes reigned.

The dimensions of the church are as follows: Length of the interior 613½ English feet, of transept from wall to wall 446½ feet; height of nave 152½ feet, of side aisles 47 feet; Width of nave 77 to 89 feet, of side aisles 33 feet; circumference of pillars, which support the Dome, 253 feet. The cupola is 193 feet in diameter. The height of the Dome from the pavement to the base of the lantern is 405 feet; to the top of the cross 448 feet.[5] (In the ball beneath the cross, I was with seven more pilgrims at the same time, and in it I wrote a postal card to America, to my brother.) The Dome is encircled and strengthened by six bands of iron. A stairway leads to the roof, broad and easy enough to allow a loaded horse to ascend. The annual cost of keeping the Church in repair is 30,000 scudi, according to our money, $6,000.

St. Peter's Church, though externally magnificent in materials and dimensions, is disfigured by the prominence of the front added by Maderno, which almost hides from the near spectator the principal feature, the vast and towering Dome; while, had the original plan of Bramante and Michel Angelo been followed, the whole Dome would have been visible from the square before the Church.

But the Dome itself and the interior of the edifice are held to be unrivalled in magnitude, proportion and decoration. About in the centre of the Church is a bronze baldachin ninety-three feet high, which is above the high Altar. Underneath this Altar is the "Confessio," around which are eighty-two lamps, burning constantly. Beneath a flight of two stairways and before the grave of St. Peter, is a beautiful statue of Pius VI, a masterpiece of Canova. It is called "Confessio" or "Martyrium" *i. e.* Confession, because the martyrer, yet in the grave as it were, through his wounds, confesses his faith in Christ.

The south part of the Church's nave contains the confessionals for the different nations. Above the confessional for the Germans for instance, we read the words: "Pro lingua germanica," and so on for each nationality. After confession the penitent comes out of the confessional, kneels down before the confessional before the priest, who with a long staff knocks the penitent slightly on the head. A special Indulgence is connected with this ceremony; it has the following meaning.

If any one in the time of old pagan Rome, wanted to set his slaves free, he was taken before the judge to the Forum, there he gave him his liberty with the last stroke, as an external sign of his liberty; this applies to the spiritual slavery of the sinner; itself gives the explanation.

---

[5] Appleton's Cyclopædia.

The large oval area in front of St. Peter's is surrounded by a superb colonade, the top of which is adorned with 110 statues, each about seven feet high. In the middle, between two fountains, is an Egyptian Obelisk, seventy-eight feet in height; on the top of it is a cross, and in the centre of it a particle of the true Cross, announcing as it were, the triumph of Christ over paganism.

On Sunday, the 17th of March, I, amongst other priests of our pilgrims, said Mass in St. Peter's. The Immense "Thesaurus" of St. Peter's Church was also shown to the pilgrims.

On Monday, the 18th of March, the pilgrims had the great honor of having an audience with the Holy Father, Leo XIII. The afternoon before, we were made acquainted with the necessary ceremonies that pertain to the audience. First Rt. Rev. Bishop Rademacher, Monsignor Seton and Very Rev. Chas. A. Vissani had audience in a parlor of the Vatican next to us (Rt. Rev. Bishop Wigger was absent on account of sickness, but had audience later on). After the old and saintly looking Pope had given audience to the above named, he came to the priests and laymen of the pilgrimage, who were all kneeling in the throne parlor of the Pope, with their religious articles, such as rosaries, crosses and crucifixes, in their hands, which the pilgrims bought in the Eternal City.

The feeling, that overwhelms every one, but especially the Catholic at this sight, can not be expressed with words. The Holy Father was in the best of humor and very glad to see the American pilgrims, as His Holiness likes the Americans especially. As His Holiness passed the pilgrims, he shook hands with most of them, continually smiling and talking in the Italian language; Father Vissani interpreting it. The Holy Father said, amongst other things, "He wished he also had the happiness of going to the Holy Land once, and that the Americans would also have an 'hospice' in Jerusalem, as have the Germans and Austrians." After this he gave us all his blessing, and then went into the next parlor to give audience to the ladies of our pilgrimage. In the mean time, each one of us received a silver medal from the Holy Father as remembrance. After the audience, the pilgrims had their photographs taken in a group, of which each one afterwards bought a picture, which, when we now look over it from time to time, recalls to our minds so many joyful events of the first American Catholic pilgrimage.

The city of Rome has 360 churches and 180 conventual edifices, but many of the convents and monasteries have been suppressed since the occupation of the city by the Italian government, and the buildings converted to public uses.

The pilgrims next visited the celebrated *Church of St. John of Lateran*, founded by Constantine. This is the Episcopal Church, or Cathedral of the Pope, and bears over its chief portal the inscription, "Omnium urbis et orbis ecclesiarum mater et caput." "Mother and head of all the churches of the city and the world." At its main altar none but the Pope can say Mass, for it covers another ancient altar at which the Apostle St. Peter said Mass.

In the adjoining palace 161 Popes lived (of whom 47 are Saints), and celebrated the highest feasts. Twenty-three Popes are buried here. There were also five general councils of the Church held here. This Church possesses the table on which the Last Supper was taken. This table is placed above the high altar on which is kept the Blessed Sacrament, besides two large particles of the true Cross and other instruments of the Passion. As soon as we enter the Church, we have in its centre before us the grand altar of the Blessed Sacrament; built with the richness of most costly and rare pillars and stones; there is no altar in the whole of Rome that excels it, on which the Holy Eucharist is kept. And it is very proper, too, that in the Mother Church and centre of all Catholic unity, the mystery of the Most High be thus honored which forms the focus of the whole soul of religion, and the bond of unity for all children of the one Father.

By going around this Church of St. John of Lateran, we at once come to the chapel of the "Scala Sancta," the Holy Stairway, which our Divine Saviour ascended after his flagellation to be placed before the people by Pontius Pilate. There is hardly a second sanctuary that speaks so tender and impressive to the heart of the Christian.

On the floor below, before we ascend the twenty-eight steps, we see two statues, one of "Judas," the other "Ecce Homo." These steps are covered with wood; between the cracks, here and there, we behold marks of the blood of Christ, over which is a glass cover. Each one of the pilgrims went up these steps, praying on each step an Our Father to gain the Indulgence. Continually we can see pious people ascending these steps on their knees. Pope Pius IX. visited these steps even the day before Rome was taken in 1870, this being the last time in his life that he left the Vatican.

The Vatican.

The pilgrims also visited the Vatican, the papal palace, so called from its situation on the Mons Vaticanus, at the extreme north-west part of the city. It adjoins the Basilica of St. Peter's, and is a little less than half a mile from the castle of Saint Angelo. The palace, one of the most magnificent in the world, has grown up by degrees and consequently exhibits a great want of architectural harmony. There certainly was a palace attached to St. Peter's in the time of Charlemagne, and probably before the reign of Constantine. It was rebuilt by Innocent III. (1198—1216), and enlarged by Nicholas III., but did not become the permanent residence of the Popes until after their return from Avignon in 1377. The Sistine Chapel was added by Sixtus IV., in 1474, and the Pauline Chapel, by Paul III., in 1534. Innocent VIII. (1484—'92) constructed the Belvedere Villa a short distance from the palace, and Julius II. (1503—'13) connected it with the Vatican by means of the celebrated loggie and a terraced court. To Julius II. is also due the foundation of the Museum. Pius VII. constructed the Braccio Nuovo for sculptures. Gregory XVI. added the Etruscan Museum, and Pius IX. has added a fourth side to the Cortile di San Damaso.

The portion of the Vatican which is now the ordinary residence of the Popes lies on the east of the loggie, and was built chiefly by Sixtus V. (1585—'90), and Clement VIII. (1592—1605). The whole palace, which is rather a collection of separate buildings than one regular edifice, occupies a space of 1,151 by 767 feet and has 200 staircases, 20 courts, and 4,422 rooms. The Scala Regia, or great staircase, is a masterpiece of Bernini, and chiefly remarkable for its perspective. It leads to the Sala Regia, built by Antonio di Sangallo as an audience hall for the reception of ambassadors and decorated with frescoes by Vasari, Marco da Siena, and others.[6]

The Sistine and Pauline Chapels

open into this hall. The former contains besides the magnificent frescoes of the ceiling, Michael Angelo's first masterpiece in painting, his "Last

---

[6] Appleton's Cyclopædia.

Judgment," together with frescoes by Perugino and others, representing passages in the lives of Christ and Moses; the latter possesses Michael Angelo's frescoes of the "Conversion of St. Paul" and "Crucifixion of St. Peter."

The "Stanze of Raphael" is the name given to four chambers decorated by the hand of that great master; the paintings in one represent events in the lives of Leo III. and Leo IV.; in another are illustrations of the sciences of theology, philosophy, poetry, and jurisprudence; in the third, the triumphs and miracles of the Church, and in the fourth, the sovereignty of the Church.

The Museum

is one of the most magnificent collections of the kind ever made. Among its principal features are the gallery of inscriptions containing over 3,000 specimens of ancient sepulchral inscriptions and monuments.

The Picture Gallery

contains greater treasures than any other in the world, though the whole catalogue barely numbers fifty paintings. Among these are Raphael's "Transfiguration," "Madonna di Foligno," and "The Coronation of the Blessed Virgin"; Domenichino's "Communion of St. Jerome."

The Library

was founded in 1378, and now contains 105,000 volumes and 25,500 manuscripts, in a building erected by Sixtus V., in 1588. The manuscript collection, though not the largest, is the most valuable in the world.[7]

The Pope's Garden.

The Pope's Garden was the next thing the pilgrims visited. We first took a good look at the horses and carriages of the Pope. We saw nothing on our

---

[7] Appleton's Cyclopædia.

whole trip in the three parts of the world, through which we traveled, to equal these carriages in splendor and beauty. Since the capture of Rome, in 1870, this garden is the only place in the open air, where the Vicar of Christ can inhale fresh air. It is a beautiful large grove of palm and other trees. In it Pope Pius IX. in the latter days of his life had a Grotto built to resemble that of Lourdes. In this garden Leo XIII. had a Pavilion built, a little beautiful cottage, in which His Holiness sometimes goes to study, as he is here unmolested. I sat in his chair.

From here the Pope has a beautiful view of St. Peter's Church. Although it is a beautiful grove, nevertheless every step he takes reminds him that he is a prisoner. His Holiness could drive out into the city, but does not feel inclined to do so. Sometimes the Cardinals drive out into the city using some of the Pope's horses and carriages.

Santa Maria Maggiore.

This is another of Rome's important churches, which the pilgrims went to see. Founder of this church is Pope Liberius, in 360. The occasion of its erection, according to a legend, was a vision. The pious senator, John Patritius, had dreamt during the night of August 5th, that he should build a church in honor of the Blessed Virgin, on that part of his property, which in the morning he would find covered with snow (Maria ad nives). On account of its grandeur this basilica received the name of Maria Major (Maria Maggiore), to distinguish it from the other churches dedicated to the Blessed Virgin. The importance of this church was yet increased, as the wood of the crib of Bethlehem was brought into it, very likely under Pope Zacharias in 750, and deposited beneath a grand altar.

The pilgrims had the great happiness to see this crib (which, without special permission, can not be seen by visitors), and kneeling down before it, venerated and touched it with their religious articles. A beautiful statue of Pius IX. is placed before it kneeling in profound veneration, as it was he, who had the crib finally placed here. This church is also in possession of a primeval picture of the Blessed Virgin, which, as is believed, was painted by St. Luke, the Evangelist, and whose veneration exceeds 1,200 years. Above the beautiful high altar is furthermore the world-renowned picture of "Our Blessed Lady of Perpetual Help."

San Lorenzo Fuori le Mura.

Two things induced the pilgrims to make a visit to this church. The grave of Pope Pius IX., who chose this for his burial place, which, through the pious offerings of the whole Christian world is most beautifully decorated, and the very extensive cemetery that surrounds this church, which, since Napoleon I., has become the common burial ground of the city of Rome. Within the city walls, only the popes are buried who wish so, and the kings of Rome.

The Pantheon.

The Pantheon, literally meaning, a temple dedicated to all the gods, was also visited by the pilgrims. This is the grandest dome that has remained for us from antiquity, which, though nineteen centuries have passed over it, still retains all its stability and magnificence. It was erected by M. Agrippa, 26 B. C., and consecrated in 608 by Pope Boniface IV., as a Christian Church, under the name of Sancta Maria Martyres, but it is still commonly called the Pantheon. It is a rotunda, 143 feet in diameter, surmounted by a dome, of which the summit is like its diameter, 143 feet above the pavement. The thickness of its walls is 17 feet at the base, 5 feet at the top and 4 feet 7 inches at the eye. The dome is built of bricks and rubble, and rests on a circular wall 20 feet thick. It has a circular opening in the top, 28 feet in diameter, otherwise no windows.

The most remarkable feature of the Pantheon is its Corinthian portico, 110 feet in length by 44 in depth, composed of 16 granite columns, with marble capitals and bases, disposed in a triple row, each column being 46 feet high and 5 feet in diameter. These columns support a pediment, a large portion of the bronze roof of which was removed by the Emperor Constantius II., and the remainder by Pope Urban VIII., to make columns for altars and cannons for the castle of Saint Angelo. Other features of the Pantheon, such as the bronze doors, 30 feet high, 10 feet wide, and 14 inches thick; the niches and ædiculæ, the marble cornice and the mosaic pavement of the interior, are in excellent preservation and give an adequate idea of the original splendor of the edifice.[8]

It contains the tombs of Raphael, the great painter, Victor Emanuel and others. In 1871 the vaults were stored with vats of petroleum and barrels of powder, the Communists intending to blow up the building, but it was taken from them on May 24th, and the explosion was prevented.

The Catacombs.

As the pilgrims also visited these I must say a few words about them to finish up with Rome. We visited the one of San Callisto. They are found in every direction outside of the walls of the city. Within a mile and a half we find no less than fifty subterranean burial places for burying the dead. It was here the first Christians, especially during the time of persecution, met to celebrate the holy mysteries and bury their dead. Connected as the Catacombs were with trials of the early martyrs of the church, their exploration and history has ever proved one of the favorite branches of research. During the time of the persecution of the Christians, commencing with that under Nero, and followed by those of Domitian, Trajan, Hadrian, Severus and Maximinus, to what is called the tenth and last persecution, which began in A. D. 303, under Diocletian. The Catacombs were crowded with those for whom there was no safety in the light of day. Each Catacomb forms a network of passages, Or galleries, intersecting each other generally at right angles, but sometimes diverging from a centre. The galleries are usually 8 feet high by 3 or 5 feet wide.[9]

The graves are in tiers on the sides and when undisturbed are found closed with marble slabs or tiles, on which are generally inscriptions or Christian emblems. On one slab we saw engravings representing the Seven Sacraments; on another, Jonas representing "Resurretion," as also a cave wherein was venerated the Blessed Virgin, (here the pilgrims sang, "O Sanctissima," and the "Magnificat,") which proves to us that the first Christians already, in the time of the Apostles, had the Seven Sacraments, believed in the resurrection and venerated the Blessed Virgin.

---

[8] Appleton's Cyclopædia.
[9] Appleton's Cyclopædia.

These now are the most important things which, amongst others, we saw at Rome. We left Rome, March 25th, on an afternoon train for Naples.

MONTE CASINO.

On our way to Naples we passed through Monte Casino, forty-eight miles north-west of Naples. From the train we saw the celebrated Monastery, established by St. Benedict, in 529, upon the mountain of the same name, 1,300 feet high. The Monastery is a massive pile, more like a palace than a convent. The interior of the church is said to surpass in beauty and costliness of decoration every church in Italy, except St. Peter's. Rev. Father Geo. Meyer, from Fryburg, Pa., one of our pilgrims, left Rome before we did, went to Monte Casino, and again met us here at the railroad station. He and I generally being room-mates he gave me the following information about Monte Casino. It belongs at present to the government, and there are about seventy students; the Benedictines must give their income to the government, it allowing each person only one frank per day.

NAPLES.

We arrived here in the afternoon about 5 o'clock on March 25th. Naples is the largest city of Italy, has 600,000 inhabitants, on the north coast of the Bay of Naples, in the immediate vicinity of Mt. Vesuvius, and ten miles from the sites of Herculaneum and Pompeii, 118 miles south-east of Rome, with which it is connected by railway. The approach to Naples from the sea is famous for its loveliness. Naples is known for its beautiful bay. The city has five principal land entrances, but it is open like New York, provided only at the leading avenues with barriers for the purpose of collecting the duties on provisions. The streets are generally straight, and paved with square blocks of lava; the large thoroughfares are lighted with gas, but only the principal ones have sidewalks. The ground story consists of a series of arched cells, all of the same shape and size, occupied generally by tradesmen, or for cafés, or restaurants, and on the upper floors lodge numbers of families.[10]

The Neapolitans live much out of doors, and it is nothing unusual to see the children being washed and dressed in the open streets. Naples has over 300 churches, the most important of them being the *Cathedral*. Over its great entrance are the tomb of Charles I., of Anjou; Charles Martel and his wife, Clementia, of Hapsburg, as also the tombs of King Andrew and of Pope Innocent IV. Opposite the entrance of the basilica, of Santa Restituta is the chapel of San Gennaro (St. Jannuarius) with the two celebrated vials that contain the blood of that Saint, the liquifaction of which gives occasion for the greatest religious festivals of Naples when the "Tomb of San Gennaro," is surrounded with the sick waiting to be cured. The tomb is under the high altar in the richly ornamented subterranean chapel, called the "Confessional of San Gennaro." Besides this cathedral, amongst other places, the pilgrims visited the grand Museum, which is the glory of Naples, and of which I shall here give a brief sketch.

THE MUSEUM.

It is situated in a building originally intended for cavalry barracks, afterwards remodeled from the designs of Fontana for the use of the University, and for some time the seat of the Academy of Science. It is still called, *Pallazzo d'egli Studii Publici,* or simply *Studii*. After the annexation of Naples by the Italian kingdom, it was named *Museo Nazionale*. It contains collections of ancient frescoes, mosaics, and mural inscriptions, Egyptian antiquities, ancient sculptures, inscriptions, bronzes, glasses, pottery, cinquecento objects, gems, medals and coins, vases, paintings, and the National Library. Among the ancient frescoes are more than 1,600 specimens found at Herculaneum and Pompeii. The collection of ancient sculpture contains the statues of the Roman emperors and a colossal bust of Julius Cæsar. The *"Room of the Papyrii,"* includes more than 1,700 rolls of writings from Herculaneum, disfigured by the effects of the fire, of which about 500

---

[10] Appleton's Cyclopædia.

have been successfully unrolled. The gallery of paintings contains 500 works, many of them masterpieces of the old painters.[11]

Pompeii.

One day we also rode to Pompeii, twelve miles south-east of Naples, by train at the foot of Mt. Vesuvius. It is a favorable summer resort for the people of Naples. It was overwhelmed by the eruption of Mt. Vesuvius, August 24th, in the year 79, after the birth of Christ. The sea formerly came up to the city walls; it is now more than a mile away from it, as the lava and ground filled that space. The deposit of ashes and cinders had an average depth of fifteen feet.

Charles III., of Naples, ordered excavations on an extensive scale, and in 1755 the amphitheatre was uncovered. His successors, including Victor Emanuel, have continued the work from time to time, until a large part of the city was brought to light. The excavation is of incalculable importance to us; it giving us an idea of the domestic economy, the arts, and the social life of the ancient world. The articles excavated were very well preserved in the lava. At the entrance of Pompeii is a kind of a museum in which are exhibited the excavated articles. When the catastrophe happened several thousand of the inhabitants were assembled in the amphitheatre. It is generally supposed that the number of inhabitants was from twenty to fifty thousand.[12]

On Leaving Naples.

After having spent three days at Naples, the pilgrims embarked for Egypt on Thursday, March 28th, at 7 o'clock P. M., on the steamer "Asia". As soon as the pilgrims came on the steamer, a great many were immediately seasick, caused partly by the tossing about on the small boat that took us out on board of the steamer "Asia", and partly on account of the foul air which was inhaled in the steamer, while all were in the saloon, or dining department, waiting for our guides to give us the numbers of our berths. There was considerable

---

[11] Appleton's Cyclopædia.
[12] Appleton's Cyclopædia.

confusion and a great deal of dissatisfaction on account of our guides not having made proper arrangements with the captain beforehand. But in a few hours most of the sick passengers were all right again.

There were almost more passengers on board of the steamer than by rights should have been, therefore the captain treated us to a very nice kind of wine, called "*Hesti-wine*," which foams more than common beer, during the meals of dinner and supper. After the steamer left Naples, and went out into the Mediterranean Sea, it being almost night, the city of Naples as well as the thousands of gas-lights around its magnificent bay afforded a most beautiful sight. As the beautiful city of Naples was lost to our view, the great Vesuvius showed us his monstrous flame of light for several hours. The next day, at about 1:30 P. M., the steamer arrived at Messina, and stopped until 3 o'clock P. M. Messina is a province of Sicily, including the north-east extremity of the island, bordering on the Mediterranean Sea and the strait of Messina, which separates it from Calabria. It has a population of about 129,000. The following morning at 8 o'clock, we saw the volcanos of Ætna and Etromboli, and they remained in view until 10 o'clock in the evening. Mt. Ætna is 10,872 feet high. The distance from Naples to Alexandria, Egypt is about 1,200 miles.

Our sailing on the Mediterranean Sea was delightful; the captain of the steamer saying: "That this trip was the finest he had made on the Mediterranean during the last twenty-five years.

On the ocean, as long as the passengers can see land, they always have something that draws their attention but when land and steamers are lost from view, and nothing but water and the firmament are to be seen, the passengers talk to each other in the most intimate manner.

While we were on the Mediterranean Sea on our voyage to Alexandria, Monsignor Seton, of Jersey City, N. J., who was always in the best of humor, sat at the same table with Mr. John Hoebing, of Wall Lake, Iowa. The Monsignor, knowing Mr. Hoebing to be a pretty smart and jovial gentleman, among other questions asked him in a jovial manner: "John, have you any Monsignors in Iowa?" Mr. Hoebing, knowing in what way the question was meant, in his smart and unpretending way of answering, said: "Well, I was at the New Orleans Exposition and there I ate mackerels, and in Italy macaronies, and I now know what lazaronies are, (beggars, of whom there are so many in Italy) but Monsignors, I don't know what that is, I wouldn't know whether to eat them with the spoon or fork". You can imagine, dear reader, if ever the old Monsignor burst out laughing, it was at this ingenious and unexpected answer.

Arrival at Alexandria, (Egypt).

After having been on the Mediterranean for five and one-half days from Naples to Alexandria, we reached the latter city safely on Tuesday morning, April 2d, at 8 o'clock. The pilot, who guided our steamer at Alexandria, did not come on the board of the steamer as they usually do, but sailed alongside of our steamer in a skiff and thus safely guided it as far as the steamer could go. Immediately some of the Franciscan priests came from the shore to meet us as did Cook's men; the latter having the word "Cook's" in large red letters, on the chest of their white overshirts, skillfully rowed us in skiffs to the shore of Egypt. As we first saw these Egyptians, whose costumes are so very much different from those of the Europeans, we were all amazed. From the way they dress, we sometimes can hardly tell a man from a woman. On coming to shore one of Cook's principal guides in Egypt came to meet us, and conducted us in carriages to the depot, where we deposited our baggage, and then drove to our hotel. Afterwards, we took a walk in the streets of Alexandria. Here in one Franciscan church the Fathers preach in five different languages, viz.: Maltese. Arabic, Italian, English and German.

ALEXANDRIA.

Alexandria, a city of Egypt, on the Mediterranean, is 112 miles north-west of Cairo, founded by Alexander the Great, after the destruction of Tyre, 332 B. C. In Alexandria the Scriptures were first made known to the heathen by the Septuagint version, and here Christianity early took root. Modern Alexandria looks rather like an Italian than an Oriental city. Large streets, along side of which are many beautiful palm, date and other tropical trees and shrubs, paved and lighted with gas, are seen in the European quarter, which abounds with fine residences. The great promenade of the Mehemet Ali Square, formerly the Square of Consuls, is the central and most animated part of the city. The city has 300,000 inhabitants, including, besides Arabs, Copts, Turks, Persians, Armenians, and Jews, 25,000 Greeks, 20,000 Italians, 15,000 French, 12,000 English Maltese, 12,000 Levantines of miscellaneous European descent, 8,000 Germans and Swiss, 8,000 various foreigners, comprising a number of American officers in the Khedive's army and American engineers and missionaries. Railways connect the city with Cairo and the Suez Canal. It is as a place of transit for passengers that Alexandria is most remarkable, the steamers to and from India, the Mediterranean, and the Levant all contributing to the prosperity of the city. There are also a great many men-of-war here.[13]

Egyptian Costumes.

As the Egyptian costumes are so different from the European or American, and consequently interesting to the reader, I shall here give you a faint idea of some before I proceed any further. The Egyptian women are veiled, the veil three or four feet long and four inches wide, and hangs from the top of the nose down to their feet; a veil also covers their head, so that nothing can be seen of their face. Immediately above their nose they have a metallic horn containing two rows of teeth as those of a saw. This horn, which is three inches in length and is made of gold, silver or brass, is fastened around the head with a string. From this horn is suspended a veil, hanging down to the feet, which hides from view the Mohammedan women. On account of the intense heat, their wearing apparel is very light, and is made from velvets, silks or cheaper woven goods, as their means may allow it. Sometimes it is hard to distinguish the men and women. The men wear long gowns called toga or burnus, made in black, white or some gay color. These togas are often very much tattered, some men even being seen in Paradise costume. Over this toga they wear a waistcoast, called kaffir, made of divers colors. They cover their heads with a skull-cap or fez, around which they wind a cloth, called turban, the color of which being a matter of taste. Those Mohammedans, however, who have made a pilgrimage to Mecca, are allowed the privilege of wearing a green turban. All wear a sash

---

[13] Appleton's Cyclopædia.

tied around their waist. Boots are not worn. The Arabians wear galoshes, low shoes or slippers, some, however, going barefooted.

The different classes of people are distinguished by their various dress. An officer v. g. wears a black burnus and a white turban, while the fellahs (poor people) wear a Denim burnus and a red turban. The so-called Tartars wear furs instead of a turban; the Armenians a yellow kaffir, and the Dervishes (Mohammedan monks) a green or gray attire.

How the Country People Live.

We left Alexandria for Cairo, the capital of Egypt, April the second, at two o'clock in the afternoon. During this journey we had a good opportunity of observing how Egytian country people live. There are about eighty villages and stopping places between Alexandria and Cairo, a distance of about 128 miles, which are often not a half mile apart. Owing to the low condition of the country, and for safety sake, the houses are built very closely together.

The railroad tracks are much narrower than in America, the ties being made of iron. The cars are of a very uncomfortable size. The telegraph posts are very low and generally made of stone. The wires are at least three times thicker than those in this country, and porcelain isolators are used. The locomotives are similar to those used in Europe.

When a train nears a station, the majority of villagers eagerly rush to the depot and offer donkeys for sale. Vendors of confectioneries, fruits, etc., are very noisy, making it impossible to hear one's own words. Villages of 600 to 800 inhabitants consist mostly of one-story buildings, built of stone, although the sheiks (chiefs) and English officers dwell in two-story houses more substantially built. As it seldom rains or gets cold, the fellahs live in small and low one-story dwellings, having one low door but no window. For protection against the rays of the sun, the roof is covered with grass or bulrush.

A village generally contains from 50 to 150 such mud houses, which are separated from each other by crooked alleys, and surrounded by a mud wall. The door answers the purpose of a chimney. Bake-oven, granary chairs and all house furniture are made of mud. In such a hut can be found neither tables, stoves nor beds, but instead of all this are troughs for sheep, donkeys, goats and camels. Children are numerous, as are chickens and different species of animals.

The manure is laid out in the sun to dry, and then is used as fuel. In one of these miserable huts often a man habitates with three or four women. Around these mud-huts sit or lie promiscuously people, camels, goats, sheep, buffalo-oxen, chickens, dogs, cats, etc., all constituting as it were one large family.

The country is irrigated by the river Nile, through machinery resembling our wind-mills and drawn by buffalo-oxen.

THE COUNTRY OF EGYPT.

Egypt is in northeastern Africa. It is bounded on the north by the Mediterranean Sea, on the east by the Red Sea and a direct line from Suez to El-Arish, which is a seaport town on the Mediterranean. There are few small rivers in Egypt which empty into the Red Sea, but the river Nile is the main irrigator of the country. For over one hundred miles, which we traversed, the country is level, the soil being rich and magnificent.

The land is intersected with numerous canals, chiefly constructed to facilitate the distribution of the water of the Nile for irrigation. To irrigate the land, the inhabitants use wooden machinery, resembling a wind-mill, to which are fastened wooden buckets, similar to our old-fashioned water-pumps. The machinery is operated by camels or buffalo-oxen.

Across the isthmus of Suez is a canal, uniting the Red Sea with the Mediterranean. This canal was begun in 1859, and opened to navigation in 1869. Granite, sandstone and limestone is principally found in this region. The richness of the soil is renewed annually by the overflow of the Nile, the inundation bringing upon the land a coating of mud, which makes all manure useless. In many parts of the country ploughing is done away with altogether, as they throw the seed upon the mud, then a large number of sheep, goats or oxen are driven upon the fields and trample the grain into the mud. The plough is constructed entirely of wood, and drawn by buffalo-oxen, who walk eight feet apart. I and a few of our inquisitive pilgrims ploughed with these miserable contraptions. In some other parts of the country, where artificial irrigation can be resorted to, considerable care and labor is bestowed upon agriculture. Sometimes the inundation reaches a height of twenty-four feet, and in this height it remains for about fifteen days. Wheat, barley, beans, peas, lentils, clover, flax, lettuce, hemp, tobacco, watermelons and cucumbers are sown immediately after the inundation subsides, and after three or four months they are harvested. Wheat is ripe in the latter part of March. By artificial irrigation they raise in summer: Durra, maize, onions, sugar cane, cotton, coffee, indigo and madder. Grapes are plentiful, as are also dates, figs, pomegranates, apricots, peaches, oranges, lemons, citrons, olives, bananas and mulberries.

CAIRO.

At our arrival at Cairo, one half of our pilgrims were taken to Hotel Shepherds, owned by Philip Zech, a German, and the other one half were taken to Hotel New, both being elegant hostelries and well conducted. Cairo is situated 120 miles, southeast of Alexandria. It numbers 400,000 inhabitants, of whom by far the largest number are Mohammedans; 70,000 Copts, and the rest chiefly native Jews, Greeks, Armenians and Europeans. It lies in the beautiful, fertile and level plain of the Nile Valley, and has a circumference of eight miles. From without it presents a grand and beautiful spectacle, but within it is not attractive. The houses of the poor people are only one-story high, and built of mud or bricks baked in the sun. The richer people have houses of brick, wood, and a soft stone quarried from the mountains of Mokattan, which are near by, some of the houses being two or three stories high. The streets are narrow, unpaved, dusty and very much neglected, although in the principal parts of the city and suburbs they are wide enough for carriages. It seldom rains at Cairo, and a heavy shower is considered almost a calamity, for then the moistened garbage, which is so abundant in the streets, undergoes speedy decomposition, the exhalations of which are pesfiferous. Another cause of disease is the stagnant water in May and June which, by means of a canal, is conveyed into the city whenever the Nile overflows. Horses are rarely employed, donkeys being mostly used. Carriages are, and can only be, used in a few streets. At hotels, or at any other public place, Arabian boys can be seen at almost any hour of the day or night with donkeys, which they offer to strangers to take them to any part of the city. Our hotel-keeper advised us not to go with them at night, as it is not considered safe.

The Arabian boy accompanies his donkey and the tourist wherever the journey leads to, and they keep pace with the donkey, their durability being nearly equal to our American horses.

There are many inns and large store-houses in Cairo. Its bazaars, some of which we visited, are very extensive, and present a good display of oriental merchandise. Its four hundred mosques are the pride of Cairo, some of which are elegant specimens of Arabian architecture. We visited the most renowned mosque, that of Sultan Hassan, which is built near the citadel. The entrance is magnificently embellished with tracery. Its interior court has no roof. There is on each side a square recess, covered with a fine arch, and towards the east a niche for praying and a pulpit, containing elegant, various colored glass vases of Syrian manufacture, which bear the Sultan's name. We also visited the mosque of Mehemet Ali, and the citadel, which affords a fine view of the city, the Nile and the pyramids.

In the center of the mosques is a water font, at which each person, who enters to worship, must wash feet and hands. When praying, the worshippers kneel, frequently touching the floor with their foreheads. They arise and often repeat the ceremony. During prayer they must all turn their faces towards a niche, which each mosque contains, and which is turned towards Mecca. Before entering a mosque, we were obliged to take off our shoes or boots and wear old and worn red slippers, which the janitor has ready for visitors at the entrance. Some of our party often lost these large slippers and, not thinking the place to be so holy, we thought that we could walk without them; but the janitor would soon be upon us, scolding and making us put them on again. The Mohammedans are more particular about their feet than their heads, as it is allowed to keep the hat on.

In one church in Cairo, services are held in eight different rites or languages.

As the different races of people, who live in Cairo, inhabit various quarters, we find the Jewish quarter, the French quarter, the Coptic quarter, etc. The entrances, which lead to the different quarters, are closed at night.

For police regulation, the city is divided into eight wards, and all officers of the city are under one chief. Each sheikh, or head, is, generally speaking, responsible for the conduct of his people. The Khedive has a theatre for French comedy and an opera house.

The immense annual pilgrimage to Mecca assembles at Cairo, and, as they carry a large stock of goods for traffic, their departure and return to Cairo is a remarkable source of wealth.

The Mohammedans place eatables upon the graves of their deceased every Thursday evening. By the next morning they have been eaten by dogs, they, however, believing that the spirits of the deceased have eaten them.

Many of our pilgrims took carriages for Heleopolis, about six miles from Cairo, to see the tree under which the Blessed Virgin is said to have rested with the child Jesus, during their stay in Egypt. We also visited a Coptic church near Cairo, where the Holy Family rested for a month, and saw the spot where the Blessed Virgin sat with the Divine Infant.

Whilst we were here, an Arabian, who had some of the horns which the Egyptian women wear, and which I described before, offered one for sale to one of our pilgrims. "Oh," said our American, "we have no wives." "Well," said the vendor, "you can get one over here for five piasters." (One piaster is equal to about five cents of our money.)

We were told that an aspirant for a preacher or priest in the Greek Church is asked three questions by his bishop. If he can write; if not, to learn it; if he has a beard; if not, to raise one; if he has money; if not, to get some. They surely do not require much.

Audience with the Khedive.

During our three days' stay at Cairo, we also had the honor of an audience with the Khedive of Egypt. Mr. Caldwell, of Texas, Tenn., American Consul at the court of Cairo at the time, procured for us this interesting audience, and kindly introduced us to the Khedive, who shook hands with each of us in a friendly manner. The consul had previously made us acquainted with the customary ceremonies. The ladies of the pilgrimage were excluded from the audience, as the women are considered by the Egyptians as slaves more or less. The Khedive Theofuz, who died January the tenth, 1892, was quite a young man of handsome appearance. In addressing us, he spoke English very well and fluently. Prince Abbas, his son, who is now the Khedive, was born July the fourteenth, 1874. He attended the university at Vienna at the time of the death of his father, and among other languages, also studied the German.

Rt. Reverend Bishop Joseph Rademacher addressed the Khedive in the name of the pilgrims in a few eloquent and well-chosen words, and also thanked His Majesty for being so kind and good to the Catholics of Egypt. During the audience, the Khedive treated us to a small cup of black coffee, which his servants brought to us on beautiful gold-plated waiters. This is considered quite a treat by the Orientals. After this, the Khedive conversed with us for quite a while; then he dismissed us by again shaking hands with each one.

THE BOULAK MUSEUM.

We next went to Boulak, one mile northwest of Cairo. This town, rebuilt by Mehemet Ali, had at one time over five thousand inhabitants, but in the eighteenth century it was burnt down by the French. Here is a museum in which the different celebrated antique collections are arranged according to their civil or religious character, the most antique being placed most conspicuously.

We saw here three statues which date back to the age of the shepherd-kings. One of the vestibules is filled with relics of the most ancient Egyptian art. Here we beheld wooden statues belonging to the fourth dynasty, and a granite statue of Cephren, who built the second pyramid. Still more interesting than all of this is the immense collection of furniture, household articles, implements used by the Egyptians, glass and earthenware, etc. This was the most curious and interesting museum we saw.

We saw here, for the first time, Egyptian mummies. A mummy is a body embalmed so as to preserve it from decay. This custom was somewhat practiced by the Persians, Assyrians, Etheopians, Romans, Hebrews and Greeks, but was mostly in use by the Egyptians, as they embalmed all their dead. The Egyptian mummies, found to-day in their sepulchres, some of which have been preserved for more than four thousand years, show us how perfectly this art was understood by them even in those remote ages. They embalmed reptiles and animals, which were held sacred by them. It seems wonderful to us whence they obtained the many drugs and spices, which were required for this process of embalming; when we learn that they embalmed all human bodies, as well as several millions of dogs, apes, crocodiles, cats, bulls, rams, foxes and other animals, in all more than fifty species.

The following is their most perfect process of embalming: They use a bent piece of iron with which the brains are taken out through the nostrils; then the skull is cleared with drugs after which a cut is made along the flank with a sharp Etheopian stone; after the intestines are taken out, they wash the cavity with palm wine, after which it is filled with pure myrrh and the opening sewed up. After this the body is covered and placed in natron for sixty days; after which the body is wrapped from head to foot with bandages of pure linen, coated with gum, and enclosed in a case made of cloth, cemented together. This is done when the body is damp, so as to get the exact shape. It is afterward sewed up in the back; then richly painted and gilded, the face either colored, so as to make it look natural, or overlaid with thick gold leaf, and eyes, made of enamel, put in. Thereupon it is enclosed in a wooden case, man-shaped, and placed in an upright position against the wall in a sepulchral chamber. The bandages, which are sometimes over one thousand yards long, differ very much in quality, coarse canvas to the finest linen being used. The features are natural, and teeth, hair and eyebrows well preserved. Mummies are easily broken as they are dried and very light.

BOAT-RIDE ON THE NILE AND DONKEY-RIDE TO THE PYRAMIDS.

The Nile is the principal river of Africa, and one of the most famous and largest of the world. From Cairo we took a twenty minutes' drive in carriages to the Nile, where we went aboard the steamer "Prince Mohamed Ali." We passed the island of Roda, where it is supposed Moses was found. We took the boat at Boolak, the port of Cairo, and went up the Nile as far as Mitrahenny. We also passed a town called Tura, from where the stones, used in building the pyramids, were taken.

Before we left Cairo, the men purchased white straw hats, and white veils which were fastened to the hat, and on account of the intense heat, also took our umbrellas with us. Our guides had ordered some Arabian boys to be in readiness for us at Mitrahenny, with their donkeys. We had brought our saddles along on the boat from Cairo, so that when we arrived at Mitrahenny we saw over one hundred donkeys. As we neared the bank, the Arabian boys waded to the boat, each one holding out his hands for a saddle. When one would be handed them from the boat they would run with it and place it on their donkey, whereupon we hurriedly followed so as to secure a donkey. The boys were very noisy, patting their donkeys and praising them to the pilgrims. The donkeys are named such as Czar Nikolaus, Grant, George Washington, Augusta Victoria, Ibrahim Mahomed, etc.

Now began the donkey-race. One after the other galloped away, the drivers running alongside, without waiting for our guides, and within a short while more than twelve of us fell to the ground, those following us falling over us. Although it was dangerous, it was also very amusing.

Finally we arrived at Memphis, the old city of the Pharaohs', which, in the time of Joseph of Egypt and the vizeroy, was a renowned place. We find ruins and excavations everywhere. At one of these ruins, the corn-crib of Joseph was shown us. We also saw a granite statue of Rameses II which he had ordered made and to be adored as God. We walked around this colossal statue, which is twenty feet in height. weighs five tons, and is well preserved. Rameses II. ordered all male children drowned in the Nile. Moses was saved by his mother placing him in a basket.

After having stopped here for fully half an hour, we again mounted the donkeys and crossed the Desert of Sakarah. We could hardly endure the heat; drinking water was not to be seen nor to be had. We made one stop at an inn, built of stone, where we partook of dinner, which our guides had brought along from Cairo.

The Serapeum.

After dinner we visited the mausoleum of the sacred bulls, which during Pharaoh's regime was a large building, but now it is completely covered with sand. After we had reached the Serapeum, or resting place of the sacred bulls, we descended a flight of sixty or seventy steps, which landed us in this immense building, which at one time was above the ground. Our guides conducted us through the principal hall, which is 700 feet long and 30 feet wide, and we were obliged to use torches so as to enable us to see. To our right and left we beheld large halls, which contained beautiful stone coffins, standing on pedestals about six by ten feet in diameter. Some of us looked into one of these sarkophagus. but could see only a few ashes.

We also went into the mines of the Sakarah pyramids and Mustaba a Ti, where the Egyptians buried their kings, which are located in the Desert of the Sakarah. From here we went a distance of fifteen miles, but which did not seem to us to be more than five, to

THE SPHINX.

"Sphinx, a fabulous monster of Greek mythology, which generally was represented as having the head and breast of a woman and the body of a lion."

The Egyptian Sphinx had the head of a man, shaved, and the body of a lion, in which way they differed from the Greek sphinxes. They were placed in front of their temples, to signify the mysterious nature of their deity.

The great Sphinx, by the pyramids, is to represent King Cephren, who built the second pyramid, but according to the inscription it was sculptured before the time of the builder of the first pyramid, Cheops.

From the top of the head to the chin, this Sphinx measures twenty-eight feet, and the body is 146 feet high. Across the shoulders it measures thirty-six feet, and the paws extend fifty feet. The paws are built of masonry, while the rest seems to have been carved from the solid rock. Between the paws a small temple was built of masonry. The Sphinx has been examined and found to be of one piece of stone. The face is at present so mutilated that the features can hardly be traced.

THE PYRAMIDS.

We next inspected the largest pyramid, that of Cheops, which is near the Sphinx. This pyramid is the largest stone structure in the world.

Pyramids are constructed of large blocks of stone, taken from the quarries of the Nile. The stones are of extraordinary dimensions; their transportation to the pyramids and adjustment in their places indicate a surprising degree of mechanical skill in those primative times, which we can hardly comprehend. The stones average two feet by four or six feet. The foundations of these pyramids were excavated in solid rock about ten feet deep; upon this foundation the large stones were laid in layers, the space being well filled out with smaller stones. These pyramids run to a point, and when they were constructed, the number of workmen must have been comparatively small for want of room. They are one of the seven wonders of the world.

The three pyramids near Memphis are about 125 feet above the highest rise of the Nile, and their four sides are directed towards the cardinal points. This pyramid of Cheops covers thirteen acres; its former height was 480 feet, but it is at present only 450 feet. The weight is estimated at six million tons. There is a passage-way on the north side, three feet ten inches high and three feet wide. It is supposed that originally sepulchral chambers for Egyptian kings were here.

Six or seven of our pilgrims ascended this pyramid, which cannot be done without the aid of guides. There are always some Arabians about, who take strangers to the top of the pyramids. Two take the traveler by the hand and one supports him from the back. This usually costs one dollar, sometimes less. There is a regular path leading up, which is known best and probably only to these guides.

After completing our inspection of the pyramids, the Arabians took their donkeys home and we took carriages for Cairo. We were glad it was over, as we were very tired of this novel ride, which was our first experiment of riding on the celebrated Egyptian donkeys in that hot sun.

We left Cairo again Thursday evening, at ten o'clock, and took the train for Ismailia.

THE BEDOUINS.

It took us eight hours before we reached our place of destination. We came through the Arabian Desert, where it is barren. Telegraph posts are made of stone, and the depots are poorly built. Upon the arrival of trains, the Bedouins and other inhabitants of the desert, rush in great numbers to the depots, offering donkeys and Arabian horses for sale.

As we here meet Bedouins for the first time. I think it not amiss to give a short description of them.

The Bedouins (dwellers of the desert) are a tribe of Arabians and also of the eastern and southeastern parts of Syria. They are found to live in tribes of about twenty thousand men, wandering from place to place, as the flocks require it. From the earliest ages they have led a pastoral life, living in tents and rearing cattle, which they sell in the cities. They plunder, and spend their leisure time in horse-racing, telling stories and smoking. The women and slaves must perform all the housework; the men milking and spinning. The land, which they own, is cultivated by the neighboring farmers, who receive one-third of the produce as a compensation for their services. The women are mostly hairdressers, and spend considerable time in curling the looks of their husbands. The children tend to the flocks. The Bedouin despises all labor, and agriculture he considers beneath his dignity. He is fierce and war-like, not for patriotism, as he claims no country, but only for the sake of plunder. Nearly every tribe has a poet, who proclaims the deeds of their heroes. They are very much attached to their horses, and are considered the best riders of the world. They live principally on rice and coffee and the flesh and milk of their flock. They abhor living in buildings, and when compelled to go to towns to sell wood, grain or cattle, they make their stay as short as possible. They are of medium height, are not easily fatigued and can stand the exposure to the greatest heat and sands of the desert. They are generally clothed only in a cotton shirt, fastened around the waist with a leather girdle. The sheikh and the wealthy wear a long scarlet shirt, carrying in their girdle their customary weapons, pistols and a short dagger. Around their heads they wear a woolen or silk shawl, embroidered with gold lace. Their boots are clumsily made of red or yellow leather. They are revengeful, superstitious and very ignorant, but at the same time are hospitable. They have a criminal code only for murder. Each tribe has its sheikh or chief, who leads them to battle and acts as arbitrator in differences. When danger threatens, they retire to their deserts, as the wells are known only to them, and it is almost impossible for their enemies to follow them.

We arrived at Ismailia, which is one hundred and fifty miles from Cairo, about five o'clock.

ISMAILIA.

Ismailia is a town of Lower Egypt, being situated on the Suez Canal. It has a population of 4,500. After having breakfasted, we took an eight minutes' walk to the Suez Canal, and immediately one-half of the pilgrims took a steamer for Port Said, on the Suez Canal. The other one-half were obliged to wait for another steamer. The Suez Canal was begun simultaneously at Port Said and at Suez, and while the work was going on, Port Said was central seat. It was called thus after the Khedive.

THE SUEZ CANAL.

The Red Sea and the Mediterranean Sea are divided by the Isthmus of Suez, which connects Africa and Asia. The Suez Canal is about 160 miles in length and about 150 steps in width, the land along the canal being only about eight feet above the sea level. The surrounding country is mostly a barren, sandy desert, and sparsely inhabited. It is supposed that the Mediterranean and the Red Sea were formerly connected and that the isthmus was under water. Two ships can easily pass each other. The Israelites, on their exodus from Egypt, are supposed to have crossed the Red Sea a short distance beyond the head of the Gulf of Suez. The canal was opened in November, 1869.

The weather was pleasant and thus we could observe everything well, on both sides of the canal. We saw only one small landing town, called Kantarah, along the whole distance from Ismailia to Port Said. We had the Continent of Asia to our right and Africa to our left. We passed several boats, which are continually at work dredging the canal of mud and the sand, which is blown in by the strong winds. The navigable water is indicated by buoys on each side. In order that the large steamers may give way to each other, certain places are marked. When two steamers pass each other, the one which goes with the tide must rack, while the other passes on.

PORT SAID.

We arrived at Port Said about twelve o'clock noon and, after having taken dinner, some of us took a walk through the town.

Port Said is a semi-European town of Egypt, at the junction of the Suez Canal with the Mediterranean Sea, and has a population of about 9,000. It has one Catholic and one Greek church. Rev. George Meyer, of Fryburg, Pa., and myself visited the Greek church and had everything explained to us. This town grew up since the construction of the Suez Canal. About one thousand ships land here annually. Outside of that there is no commerce. Vehicles are not seen in Port Said and everything is carried. Here we saw so-called water-carriers for the first time. They sew the hides of donkeys or goats together, tie straps around them, place them around their shoulders, and thus they perform a corporal work of mercy, provided they are paid. If they have lemonade to sell in these donkeys, they clap two shells together to draw attention. An American or European must indeed be very thirsty before he will drink from such a costly and tasteful vessel.

About five o'clock in the evening we left Port Said on the steamer "Sheikiah," for Jaffa, in the Holy Land.

JAFFA.

We had a most pleasant time on the Mediterranean Sea to Jaffa. The pilgrims were in such a good humor that they were on deck and sang during the whole evening. It sounds most beautiful on the sea, especially at night when the sea is calm. At daybreak of the next morning Jaffa was in sight. Our captain said that at Jaffa steamers could not land at all times, but have to wait until the waves subside. This is one of the most dangerous landing places in the world. On that account it has no jetties, so that vessels stop about one thousand steps or more from the land. Along the harbor is a reef of rocks, forming a kind of natural breakwater, which shelters boats and small vessels.

Cook's men immediately came in seven small boats to take us and our baggage ashore. Jaffa boatmen are very noisy; they seem to think that the more noise and gesticulations they make and the louder they shout, the more passengers they will get. A person seeing them for the first time, and who is unacquainted with their customs, would not know what it is all about.

We were also met at the steamer by some Franciscan Fathers from Jaffa, and Brother Bernardin, O. S. F., from Jerusalem, who then accompanied us through Palestine. As soon as we put foot on the Holy Land, some kissed the ground. We were obliged to pass the custom officials, but they were very lenient towards us. Our guide, Mr. Jannilly, an Italian, immediately conducted us to the Franciscan convent, where we were received with the greatest hospitality. After a little while he took us to the Greek church of St. Joseph's Orphan House, the bazaars, the house where St. Peter had the vision of the pure and impure animals, and also to the house where he resuscitated Tabitha.

It is at Jaffa (the Joppe of the ancients) where the pilgrims generally enter the Holy Land. It is about forty miles southeast of Jerusalem, and passes for one of the most ancient cities in the world. According to tradition (when in the future I use the word tradition, I mean human, not divine tradition) it existed before the deluge. It is picturesquely situated on a round hill. It is a labyrinth of blind alleys and delapidated streets, which are narrow and dirty, although from a distance the city looks well. The aspect of the city is sad and silent. It has only two gates, both opening towards the east. The number of inhabitants is as follows: 350 Latins, 375 United Greeks, 50 Maronites, 700 Schismatic Greeks, 10 Schismatic Armenians, 10 Protestants, 400 Jews, and 4,300 Musselmen.

It was here where Noah built the ark, as God had commanded him; destroyed by the waters of the deluge, it was rebuilt by Japhet (son of Noah); hence it was called Jaffa. Jonah came here to embark, in order to fly from Tharsis, far from the Lord, who had commanded him to go to Ninaveh. It was at Jaffa where Hiram, King of Tyre, embarked the timber, cut on Mount Libanus, to be sent to Solomon, which was to be used in the construction of the temple, built in honor of the true God. It was from here that the apostles went forth into the different parts of the world to preach the Gospel, as the Divine Master had commanded them.

We left Jaffa, in covered spring wagons, for Ramleh, on Saturday, April 6th, at one o'clock in the afternoon.

In 1867, under the government of Nazif Pasha, Governor of Jerusalem, a road from Jaffa to the Holy City was commenced at the cost of the inhabitants of the district, to serve as a road for riding and for light carriages. Since we were there, however, a railroad has been built from Jaffa to Jerusalem.

I, for my part, am not in favor of railroads in the Holy City, for in course of time the whole aspect will be changed. I admit that railroads make traveling easier. I would also rather have taken a train to Jerusalem and other places (although the accommodations are very poor) than fall off donkeys or to be tossed around on those wagons to Jerusalem. If we see Jerusalem now, we see it almost as it looked in the days of Christ; no rolling-mills, smoke-stacks, foundries, engines, depots and railroads. Of course, like all other things, this has its pro and contra, to some extent at least.

Leaving Jaffa.

As we got beyond the Jaffa gate, the road led in a southeastern direction, and we passed a large market with all kinds of productions, such as oranges, citrons, pomegranates, bananas, sugar canes, etc. This market is so crowded that drivers must pay close attention that their horses do no damage, and to avoid disputes and quarrels, which Orientals like very much to cause. After we had passed the market, the highroad led by gardens, which were remarkable for their fertility. The greater number of them are filled with orange and lemon trees and pomegranates.

After a ride of fifteen minutes, we reached a beautiful fountain of potable water, in a square, in which were planted cypress and sycamore trees. It is believed that in a garden to the north of this fountain, was situated the residence of Tabitha, restored to life by St. Peter. (Acts of the Apostles; chap. ix, v. 36: "And in Joppe there was a certain disciple named Tabitha; this woman was full of good works and alms-deeds which she did." V. 38: "And forasmuch as Lydda was nigh unto Joppe, the disciples, hearing that Peter was there, sent unto him two men to come unto them." V. 39: "And Peter, rising up, went with them; and when he was come, they brought him into an upper chamber." V. 40: "And, they all being put forth, Peter, kneeling down, prayed, and turning to the body, he said: 'Tabitha, arise.' And she opened her eyes and, seeing Peter, she sat up." V. 41: "And, giving her his hand, he lifted her up.")

Leaving this fountain to the right, we continued for about fifteen minutes, still passing through gardens, and, after having crossed a little stone bridge, we entered the lovely plain of Saron, which resembles a carpet of flowers at this time of the year. This fertile plain gives, alternately one year an abundant harvest, and the next, rich pasturage, with countless beautiful flowers, among which we find tulips and acnemonies. It is celebrated as the spot where Samson burnt the harvest of the Philistines by letting loose three hundred foxes with lighted torches tied to their tails. (Judges; chap. xv, v. 4: "And he

(Samson) went and caught three hundred foxes and coupled them tail to tail, and fastened torches between the tails." V. 5: "And setting them on fire, he let the foxes go, that they might run about hither and thither; and the flames consumed also the vineyards and the olive-yards")

After riding twenty-five minutes longer, we passed a small tower—a small stone house—of which we saw several along the road from Jaffa to Jerusalem. They are guard-houses, and were built in 1860, by order of Sureya, Pasha of Jerusalem. There are two or three soldiers, called Bachibouzouk, stationed here to guard the road and prevent brigandage. Further on, to the left, we passed a little village, consisting of a few miserable huts, built on a sandy soil. At a distance, towards the south, near Ramleh, we saw the tower of the forty martyrs. After driving along for forty minutes longer, we came to Lydda.

LYDDA.

Lydda has a Latin missionary, 55 Catholics, 1940 Schismatic Greeks, a few Prostestants, and about 4,000 Mussulmen. It was here that the Apostle Peter cured the paralytic Eneas. (Acts of Apostles; chap. ix, v. 32: "And it came to pass that Peter, as he passed through, visiting all, came to the saints who dwelt at Lydda." V. 33: "And he found there a certain man named Eneas, who had kept his bed for eight years, who was ill of the palsy." V. 34: "And Peter said to him: 'Eneas, the Lord Jesus Christ healeth thee! Arise and make thy bed.' And immediately he arose." V. 35: "And all that dwelt at Lydda and Saron saw him, who were converted to the Lord.")

After being about thirty minutes' ride from Lydda, we reached the convent of the Franciscan Fathers of the Holy Land, at Ramleh.

RAMLEH.

Ramleh is the ancient Arimathea, and the country of Joseph of Arimathea, who helped bury our Lord. (Gospel of St. John; chap. xix, v. 38: "After these things, Joseph of Arimathea besought Pilate that he might take away the body of Jesus . . . " V. 42: "There therefore . . . they laid Jesus.") In 1296 the

Franciscans established themselves in a private house at Ramleh in order to evangelize the people and lodge pilgrims.

Ramleh is a dirty town of 4,000 inhabitants, divided into 3,000 Mussulmen, 400 Schismatic Greeks, 100 Catholics, and a few Protestant families.

After we had taken a little refreshment with the Franciscan Fathers, we visited the tower of the forty martyrs, situated ten minutes west of the convent. It was built in 1310 by the Sultan of Egypt, Mahomet, son of Kalaoun, upon the site of an ancient church, whose name it bears, and dedicated to the forty martyrs, who died under the reign of Lucinus, at Sebaste, in Armenia, in the beginning of the fourth century. On our way to this tower, we for the first time saw lepers; twelve of these unfortunates sitting in the grass and stretching out their mutilated hands at us for "bakchiche" (money), which expression we had occasion to hear very often during our stay in Palestine. Some of our party threw some money to them, so that they would not follow us, as leprosy is contagious. There are various kinds of leprosy. These lepers were afflicted with the so-called dry leprosy. Some of them had mutilated fingers and toes, some of them being entirely eaten away; others had no nose or were mutilated in some other part of the body.

After we arrived at the tower, which is about one hundred feet high, some of us ascended it to the top, from whence we had a magnificent view, through our telescopes, of the country along the sea to the mountains of Judea. Near by is an old church of St. John from the first century. Returning from the tower, we visited the bazaars.

The next morning, it being Passion Sunday (April 7th), we said Early Mass, after which we continued our journey. Along the road, some of our wagons stopped for a short time; during which time we went to some Mussulmen, who were ploughing in this stony prairie with oxen and Arabian Libidda (ploughs). Although it was Sunday, we tried their new kind of ploughs. These Mussulmen keep their Sabbath on Friday.

LATROUM.

After we had journeyed eastward for nearly an hour, we came to a small spring and a hill called Latroum. Here the plain of Saron ends and the mountains of Judea begin. The hill is covered with ruins, which appear to be very ancient; it is inhabited by some poor cultivators (fellahs) and by two Bachibouzouks, who occupy the guard-tower. Tradition places here the residence of Dismas, the Egyptian, surnamed the good thief, because he was converted on the cross. (Gospel of St. Luke; chap. xxiii, v. 42: "And he said to Jesus: 'Lord, remember me when Thou shalt come into Thy kingdom!'" V. 43: "And Jesus said to him 'Amen, I say to thee, this day thou shalt be with me in Paradise'")

Ten minutes farther, to the left of Latroum, is situated Emmois, the ancient Emaus, celebrated for the battle of Judas Macchabeus against Georgius, King of Syria. After having proceeded for another hour, we reached a stone bridge, built across the torrent Terebinthe, whence David took five stones, wherewith to fill his sling against Goliath, whom he killed in the valley. (I. Kings; chap. xxi, v. 9: "And the priest said: 'Lo, here is the sword of Goliath, the Philistine, whom thou slewest in the Valley of Terebinth!'") In this torrent, some of our pilgrims gathered some large stones, which they, however, discarded again, after having carried them along for awhile, knowing that at the holy places they would get more precious mementos than these worthless stones, which came down from the mountains. Here we took some lunch and stopped for about two hours.

Some Franciscan Fathers from Jerusalem came to meet us here, and told us that we would have to stay here for some time, as the Schismatic Greeks would not let us enter the Holy Sepulchre Church before five o'clock, as they themselves had service until then. They also told us that those Greeks would not allow us to enter the church with the cross on our American banner (this banner I described in the beginning of this book); so I helped Father Vissany take the cross off.

We did not care to stay here that long, as we knew that we were only a short distance from Jerusalem, and were very anxious to be there. Finally we continued our journey up the hill, expecting to see Jerusalem every moment. Many of us stepped from the wagons and ran ahead, picking flowers along the road. Not seeing the Holy City, we were finally tired out, walking in the hot sun; so we told our drivers to stop and take us along again. At last we could tell that we were near Jerusalem, on account of the great number of people who met us. Only a few moments longer and behold, we see Jerusalem, the principal aim of our pilgrimage, before us. Words are inadequate to express the feelings of a Catholic, when, for the first time, he sees the Holy City.

Our Entry into Jerusalem.

Now we stopped and six or eight of our Arabian guides, who met us at Jaffa and accompanied us on our tour through Palestine, took our valises in care and brought them to the Franciscan hospice, "Casa Nuova." The American consul met us here and told us to place the cross upon our banner; that he would see us through all right. We now formed a procession, headed by our banner, carried by Rev. George Meyer, and thus we marched into the Holy City through the gate called by Europeans, "Gate of Jaffa," and by the inhabitants, "Gate of Bethlehem," or of Hebron, chanting the CXXI. Psalm:

1. I rejoiced at the things that were said to me: "We shall go into the house of the Lord."
2. Our feet were standing in thy courts, O Jerusalem!
3. Jerusalem, which is built as a city, which is compact together.
4. For thither did the tribes go up, the tribes of the Lord.
5. Because their seats have sat in judgment, seats upon the house of David.
6. Pray ye for the things that are for the peace of Jerusalem and abundance for them that love thee.
7. Let peace be in thy strength, and abundance in thy towers.
8. For the sake of my brethren and of my neighbors, I spoke peace of thee.
9. Because of the house of the Lord, our God, I have sought good things for thee.

Thus, at last, we entered the Holy Sepulchre Church, where we were received by some Franciscan Fathers and little Arabian Mass-boys, who joined in with our singing and surprised us all with their loud and clear voices. They conducted us to the Holy Sepulchre, which is in the center of the church; where Rt. Rev. Bishop Joseph Rademacher addressed us with a few touching words, saying that "we are now kneeling at the Holy Sepulchre, and should thank Almighty God for having so graciously repaid us for the hardships which we had endured on our journey and we should praise Him now for this inexpressible blessing." After this, we all, two or three at a time, entered the costly chapel of the Holy Sepulchre, knelt down, venerated and kissed the Holy Grave, of which Isaias says: "And His grave shall be glorious." A Schismatic Greek monk was standing at the Holy Grave, watching us closely. Some of us laid money on the Holy Sepulchre. Afterwards, the Franciscan Fathers in the "Casa Nuova" told us that we should not have done that, as the Greek monk took it all.

We then repaired to the Chapel, where the Blessed Sacrament is kept and after Benediction with the Blessed Sacrament, we went to the Casa Nuova, the Franciscan Monastery, where our valises were handed us and our rooms shown to us. This was our home during our stay in Jerusalem, and these Fathers deserve all praise for their kind attention.

We were in and around Jerusalem from Passion Sunday, April the 7th, until Easter Monday, April the 24th.

HISTORY OF JERUSALEM.

Jerusalem is holy for the Jews, who formerly had their temple here and who still venerate the stones, which remind them of it; holy for the Christians because Our Lord here began and terminated the salvation of mankind; precious to Mussulmen, who have built the Mosque of Omar, containing the stone on which, according to them, Jacob reposed when he saw the mysterious ladder.

Jerusalem, the ancient Salem (peace) was, it is believed, founded by Melchisedech, king and priest of Salem. (Genesis; chap. xiv, V. 18: "But Melchisedech, the king of Salem, bringing forth bread and wine, for he was the priest of the Most High God.)" Towards the year 2023, fifty years after, Salem fell into the hands of the Jebuseens, decendants of Jebus, son of Chanaan. Jebus and Salem, Jebusalem, hence the name Jerusalem (vision of peace). The Jebuseens enjoyed the blessings of peace for about five-hundred years, until Israel was delivered from bondage (B. C. 2553). About this time,

Josue conquered the promised land and almost exterminated the inhabitants, killing thirty-one of their kings. Among these was Adonisedec, king of Jerusalem. By this victory, the Israelites entered Jerusalem and inhabited it, together with the Canaanites, but the city remained exclusively to the Jebuseens, until David made himself master thereof, during the eight years of his reign. He made it his residence and the capital of his kingdom. He placed the Ark of the Covenant there in 1047 B. C. David having sinned by taking a census of his people, God punished him. Ten tribes separated from Roboam, son and successor of Solomon. For three centuries the weakened kingdom of Jerusalem had to sustain the successive invasions of the Egyptians, Philistines and several Arabian nations. Under the reign of Sedecias, 399 years before the coming of Christ, and 413 years after Solomon had laid the foundation of the temple, Nabuchodonozor came and destroyed it, and led the people captive to Babylon; 72 years later, Cyrus gave permission to rebuild the temple, which was completed in the tenth year of the reign of Darius, 511 years B. C. After Palestine was conquered by the Romans, the celebrated temple of Jerusalem was burnt and the city destroyed by the Roman soldiers. It was rebuilt by Adrian, who named it "Elia Capitolina." A. D. 326, St. Helena adorned the Holy Sepulchre and built a basilica there. Her son Constantine restored to the city its ancient name. In 614, Chosroes II. ravaged the city and destroyed the church of the Holy Sepulchre. In 637, it fell under the dominion of Omar, but he gave ample liberty to the Christians. He built a mosque which was given his name and which still bears it.

At the beginning of the ninth century, Harounel-Raschid solemnly sent the keys of the church of the Holy Sepulchre to Charlemagne. In 1099 the Crusaders took possession of Jerusalem, but before the lapse of a century the Holy City fell into the hands of Saladin, who made his solemn entry into Jerusalem in 1187, when 100,000 Christians left it. In 1222 the Franciscans were established there. From that time until the days of Ibrahim, son of Mehemet Ali, the Christians at Jerusalem have been oppressed by the Mussulmen. From the days of Solomon to the death of Christ, Jerusalem had within its walls three mountains. Under the reign of Claudius (10 years after the death of Christ) Herode Agrippa laid the foundation of a new boundary wall, enclosing Mount Bezetha and the mount now called the Christian quarter, designated by Jeremiah under the name of Garib. This wall began at the tower of Hippicos, situated to the west of the city, and reached to the tower of Sephinos, forming the north-eastern angle of the city; thence it went eastward, joining the tower situated at the corner of the royal caverns. (Considerable of this wall still exists together with a gate almost entirely buried beneath and which serves as the foundation for the gate to Damascus). Thence it continued, crossing the royal caverns towards the Cedron and southward, joining the ancient walls of the city. So we now find Jerusalem seated on five mountains: Acra, (the tower town); Sion, (height or elevated place); Moria, (chosen locality); Bezetha, (new town); and Gareb, (quarter towards the setting sun).

Jerusalem, which in the time of Alexander the Great had about 150,00 inhabitants, has to-day hardly 38,000; of these there are about 3,000 Catholics, 10,000 Jews, and the rest Musselmen, Greeks, Copts, Maronites, Armenians, etc.[14] The difference in time between Jerusalem and New York is about 9 hours, the time of Jerusalem being that much earlier.

Services in the Holy Sepulchre Church.

Six different nations, each with their own peculiar rite, officiate in the Basilica of the Holy Sepulchre: the Franciscans (Latins); schismatic Greeks; schismatic Armenians; Copts; Abyssinians or Etheopians, and Syrians. The five last mentioned are not Catholics. The four first-named nations have their own particular chapels. As the gates or doors are usually closed and the Turks hold the keys, the religious within can not go out as they please, nor cummunicate with those outside, unless by means of a sort of grating in the door, through which they receive their food.

The Franciscans have their residence or convent and chapel in the Basilica of the Holy Sepulchre, northward of the Holy Sepulchre. Those of us who said Mass on the Holy Sepulchre had to go into the church of the Holy Sepulchre and sleep there in the convent of the Franciscans the night before. The Greeks have their chapel to the east of the tomb of Our Lord; the Armenians, south, over a part of the gallery and the Copts are close to the Holy Sepulchre, and have two or three chambers to the west, which they use

---

[14] Brother Lievin de Hammt, Guide to the Holy Places.

as their dwellings. The Latins, Greeks, Armenians and Copts have each a respective right to burn lamps before the front and within the interior of the Sepulchre, at the anointing stone and before some pictures in the Basilica. On Calvary this privilege belongs exclusively to the Franciscans and Greeks. The Superiors of the Greek and Armenian monks alone have the right to exact from the Turks the public opening of the gates, of the Basilica of the Holy Sepulchre on their particular feasts, and whenever necessary, each time for a trifling remuneration of either money, coffee or wax lights, to be given to the Turks who are on guard during the time the church remains open. For this purpose they have a divan to the left of the entrance of the Basilica. The Franciscans can celebrate daily three Masses on the Holy Sepulchre. The religious doing duty at the Holy Sepulchre, make daily a procession to the different sanctuaries enclosed within the Basilica.

CALVARY AND THE HOLY SEPULCHRE.

Tradition teaches us that the ancient Judea was inhabited by Adam, who took refuge there on being banished from the terrestrial paradise, and that likewise it was this land that received the mortal remains of the first man. His head was buried in a place called Cranion (Calvary or site of the skull). For about 4000 years hell saw with delight the proofs of its victories, placed in Calvary; but in the same place its standard was destroyed and its power lost forever. There the key of heaven showed itself, the tree of victory was raised, our slavery ended and our liberty was declared; Jesus dying there, purchased for us life. Jesus was buried near Calvary in a new Sepulchre. The third day the Saviour came forth alive, thus conquering death. Christianity made rapid progress. Calvary and the Holy Sepulchre, whence the Son of God arose again, were in great veneration. Forty years later, Titus came to besiege the guilty city, stained with the murder of its God. Simon, called also the brother of Our Lord, was then bishop of Jerusalem; when he saw that the days of persecution, foretold by Our Lord, had arrived, he fled with the Christians to Pilla, beyond the Jordan, to allow the anger of God to pass by, and returned after the departure of Titus, to take possession of the ruins of Jerusalem. Calvary and the tomb of Our Lord were again open to veneration.

Fifty years later, Adrian, wishing to prevent the Christians from venerating these precious monuments of Christianity, buried the Holy Sepulchre beneath a mass of stones and rubbish, had the surface paved over, and erected thereon a temple in honor of Venus, and on Calvary he placed the idol of Jupiter. 206 years later, the emperor Constantine had the temple destroyed and demolished the idol of Jupiter. He had the Holy Sepulchre magnificently adorned, paved the square around it with handsome stones and erected three galleries here. Near the tomb he built a Basilica, which, according to his orders, should surpass in splendor and magnificence all other edifices of the time. St. Macaire, then bishop of Jerusalem, took charge of the fulfillment of the royal wishes, and in 10 years the work was completed. The Basilica included within its walls Calvary, the Holy Sepulchre and the surrounding Sanctuaries.

In the year 614, Chosroes II., king of Persia, conquered Heraclius, took possession of the Holy City, carried away the True Cross, pillaged the city and destroyed the churches, among them that of the Holy Sepulchre, carrying with him many Catholics into captivity. After the departure of the Persians, the Christians rebuilt their temples. The reconstruction of the Basilica of the Holy Sepulchre was undertaken by a monk, named Modestus, afterwards bishop of Jerusalem, and, with the aid of the patriarch of Alexandria, John the Almoner, it was completed in 15 years. Modestus could not, like Constantine, enclose within one building all the Holy Places, but erected upon each venerated spot a church or chapel, according to his means.

Ten years later, Heraclius conquered the king of the Persians, delivered the captive Christians and obliged the successor of Chosroes to return the True Cross, and he carried the precious burden on his shoulders to Calvary, through the streets of Jerusalem. barefooted, and followed by his soldiers. This was the origin of the feast of the Exaltation of the Holy Cross.

Shortly after, this precious relic was sent by the archbishop Sergius, to Constantinople. Eight years afterwards, the disciples of Mahomet conquered Heraclius, master of Syria and Persia, and besieged Jerusalem. The patriarch Sophronius, at the head of the inhabitants, by a vigorous resistance obtained a capitulation. Omar came almost alone to Medina, with only the simple equipage of an Arab chief. He concluded a treaty before the gates of the Holy City, which guaranteed to the Christians the possession of their churches and liberty of worship upon paying a certain tribute; this was about the year 636.

From this time until the beginning of the eleventh century, the Church of Jerusalem had divers alternatives of peace and persecution. The happiest reign was that of Haroun-el-Raschid, 786-807. The Christians, under this caliph had some years of tranquillity. The emperor of the West sent abundant alms to the Holy Land to repair the churches, and founded a convent, which for many years gave protection and hospitality to pilgrims of the Latin churches. Twice, during the tenth century, the Mussulmen set fire to the church of the Holy Sepulchre. But the churches were restored about the same year they were destroyed. "Then," says Raoul Glaber, "came from all parts an immense crowd of pilgrims, bringing money for the restoration of the temples of the Lord."

In 1099, the crusaders seized the Holy City, and the first care of Godfrey was, to place at the Holy Sepulchre 20 canons, to whom he gave considerable possessions. Some years later, the crusaders began to work and re-united in one monument all the isolated sanctuaries, which had been separated since the destruction of the Basilica of Constantine. Since 1244 the Franciscans, who sing night and day the divine office, replaced the number of canons.

In 1808, a fire originated in the church of the Holy Sepulchre, destroying principally the grand dome which covered the Holy Tomb, and which had been erected by the Franciscans in 1555; the dome and marble columns were replaced after the fire by ignoble and rude masonry, under the direction of the Greeks, who, by vast expenditure, obtained this power.

Now, there are some who dispute the locality of Calvary by saying: "Jerusalem was destroyed and Christ was crucified outside the city, and to-day Mount Calvary and the Holy Sepulchre are in the city walls." It is true, Jerusalem and the Holy Places were destroyed and also the Christians banished, as stated above, but there were always some Christians living in and near Jerusalem, and the banished returned after some years, and how is it possible that they could or did loose sight of those Holy Places that were so dear and precious to all. The disciples of Christ and the holy women at Jerusalem, and especially His sorrowful Mother, certainly looked for those holy spots and visited them frequently, where their Divine Master was crucified and buried. They were also very important to the apostles, because they should and did preach the crucifixion of Christ everywhere. Furthermore, the city was never completely destroyed, as there were always some towers and ruins of the old walls remaining, by which the apostles were guided. It is also said, that the second wall, which at the time of Christ cut off the city towards the north, and not the east but the west of the present Holy Sepulchre church and thus want to prove that the ground, where now stands this Basilica, was inside the city, whilst according to the apostles, it was outside the city. No one to-day can maintain with accuracy, which course this second wall took. Finally, it is said, that Christ was crucified on a mountain, and that that, which is pointed out to-day, is no mountain, not even much of a hill. To this I answer: "None of the four Evangelists who speak about Calvary, call it a mountain. I here leave one after the other of them come and speak for themselves. (St. Matth. chap. xxvii, V. 33: "And they came to the place that is called Golgatha, which is the place of Calvary." St. Mark, chap. xv, V. 22: "And they bring Him into the place called Golgatha, which being interpreted, is, the place of Calvary." St. Luke, chap. xxiii, V. 33: "And when they were come to the place which is called Calvary, they crucified Him there; and the robbers, one on the right hand, and the other on the left." St. John, chap. xix, V. 17: "And bearing His own cross, He went forth to that place which is called Calvary, but in Hebrew, Golgatha.")

DESCRIPTION OF THE INTERIOR OF HOLY SEPULCHRE CHURCH.

During our stay at Jerusalem, a Franciscan, priest and Bro. Bernardin who had met us at Jaffa, showed us the church of the Holy Sepulchre. We entered the Basilica at the principal entrance, on the south side. The first sanctuary we met was the stone of unction, which is about 15 feet from the entrance and raised about 6 inches from the ground. It measures about 8 feet in length, 4 feet in width, and 5 inches thick, around which are continually burning 8 lamps. It is a red stone of the country. Joseph of Arimathea and Nicodemus, after having taken the body of Our Lord down from Mount Calvary, placed it here on a stone in order to anoint the body of Christ before burying it, according to the Jewish custom. This sanctuary is venerated alike by Latins, Greeks, Armenians and Copts, who all burn lamps and wax candles here. About 30 feet to the west of this stone of unction we saw a round iron cage which indicates the spot where the holy women stood, whilst Joseph of

Arimathea and Nicodemus anointed the body of Our Lord. About 30 feet hence, in the centre of a rotunda, we see the chapel of the Holy Sepulchre.

This chapel, built over the grave of Our Lord, is 26 feet long, 36 feet high, including the dome, and 18 feet in width. It is built of polished native yellow stone, the front of which is ornamented with carved marble and lime-stone columns and numerous silver and brass lamps, wax candles and pictures. In this chapel 15 lamps burn continually; the 5 middle ones belonging to the Franciscans; the 5 to the right, to the Schismatic Greeks; the 4 to the left, to the Armenians and the 1 to the Copts.

On the front of the outside of this chapel 43 lamps burn continually: the 13 in the centre belong to the Franciscans; the Greeks have 4 to the right and 4 to the left, and five between those of the Franciscans and the Armenians, who have 13 between the 4 on the left side belonging to the Greeks and 5 of theirs near the Franciscans; the Copts have only 4, placed between those of the Greeks on the right side and the Franciscans.

On each side of this chapel is a small aperture, through which, on Holy Saturday the Holy Fire is dealt out to the pilgrims by the Greek patriarchs within. Of this ceremony I will speak later. The chapel is divided into two compartments; the front chamber is the "Chapel of the Angel," the compartment where the angel sat on the stone which he rolled away from the door of the sepulchre. In the center of this apartment is a part of the stone; the other part has been placed by the Schismatic Armenians in the Convent of Caiphas, outside of the Zion gate. We pilgrims saw it when visiting that convent. In the second chamber, which is reached by a low, narrow doorway, about four feet high and two feet wide, is the tomb of Christ, which is to our right, occupying the whole length and nearly half the width of the apartment. It is raised about three feet from the floor and is covered by a slap of marble about eight feet long and two feet wide, the surface and edges of which have been worn off by kisses and embraces of the pilgrims who for centuries have gathered here from all parts of the world. In this Holy Sepulchre every priest of our pilgrimage, including myself, said Mass.

The north side (in the interior) of the Holy Sepulchre is separated by three divisions, which are adorned by the denomination to which they belong. The middle division, which is decorated by a bas-relief, carved in white marble and resembling the resurrection, belongs to the Schismatic Greeks; the one to the right has a painting on the same subject, which belongs to the Armenians (not Catholic), and the one to the left has a similar painting and representation, which belongs to the Franciscans. The entrance to the Greek chapel is on the outside of the Holy Sepulchre, about twenty-five feet to the east; it is richly adorned and profusely gilded. This chapel may be called the nave of the Basilica, but is now separated from the aisles by high walls, said to have been built by the Greeks. It is quadrangular in shape, and in size forty by seventy feet. At the eastern end is the High Altar, reached by four steps and divided by a richly-gilt screen. To the right is the throne of the Greek patriarch. In the center a small globe indicates the center of the earth. The Greeks have no organs in their churches, but instead, several metallic shells which they beat together. To the west of this Greek chapel, in the rear and adjoining the Holy Sepulchre, is the chapel of the Copts. West of the entrance to the chapel is a chapel, belonging to the Syrians (Jacobites).

From here we enter the sepulchral vault of Joseph of Arimathea; here we see four funeral sites, two of which are closed and the other two are unfinished. Tradition tells us that this holy man, after having buried our Lord upon his own burial-place, wished that he and his family might repose near thereto (which is possible as this was his property), and so he had this vault built for himself and his family. About thirty feet north of the Holy Sepulchre is the Chapel of St. Mary Magdalena, where our Lord appeared to her under the form of a gardener. A figure in the circular marble pavement designates the holy place. Near by and to the north of the Chapel of St. Mary Magdalena, we ascend by four steps to the church of the Franciscans, where they recite the Divine Office day and night. According to tradition, the Blessed Virgin never left the Holy Sepulchre from the time her Divine Son had been placed therein, but she stood at some distance on account of the soldiers that guarded it. The risen Saviour showed Himself to her in this place, called on that account Chapel of the Apparition. This chapel contains three altars. The Blessed Sacrament is kept on the High Altar. The altar to the right is called Altar of Relics (on this altar I celebrated Mass on Easter Sunday), so named because a piece of the true cross was venerated here until the year 1557, when the Franciscans were imprisoned by Soliman and the Armenians, who seized this precious relic and sent it to Armenia. The altar to the left, which is the first upon entering, contains a portion of the pillar whereon our Lord was scourged; it is of porphyry and about three feet high. Once a year, on Wednesday of Holy Week, the railed door is opened and the people allowed to see, venerate and kiss the pillar. We pilgrims had this happiness on Wednesday of the Holy Week during our stay in Jerusalem.

Upon leaving the Chapel of the Apparition, we went to our left into the sacristy of the Franciscans or Latins, where are preserved the spurs and sword of Godfrey de Bouillon. As to the authenticity of this, the Franciscans received them as such from the bishop of Nazareth about the close of the thirteenth century. The spurs are made of copper, with immensely large wheels; the sword is straight and plain at the hilt. In this sacristy we of course vested when we said Mass in Holy Sepulchre Church. From this chapel we went to the left, toward the north, where is a dark chapel, belonging to the Schismatic Greeks, built, according to tradition, over the spot which was formerly a grotto, where our Lord and the thieves were imprisoned, whilst preparations for the execution were being made. This chapel contains three compartments, designating the cell of each prisoner. As we went on about thirty feet in a south-western direction, we came to a chapel also belonging to the Greeks, which is dedicated to Longinus, who, according to tradition, was the soldier who pierced the side of our Lord with a spear and, impressed by the prodigies he witnessed, that he confessed the Divinity of Christ and here bewailed his faults. (Gospel of St. John, chap. xix, v. 34. "But one of the soldiers with a spear opened His side and immediately there came out blood and water.") When Longinus made the wound, which opened the sacred side of Our Lord, the blood and water flowed down the handle of his spear, moistening the sacrilegious hand. Longinus was blind on one eye and miracuously recovered his sight by touching the eye with this hand. In this chapel was formerly venerated the inscription, placed over the cross; this precious relic is now at Rome. (Gospel of St. John, chap. xix, v. 19: "And Pilate giving a title, also put it upon the cross; and the writing was: 'Jesus of Nazareth, the King of the Jews.'")

On the same side about ten feet further on is the Armenian Chapel, built on the spot where the executioners divided Our Lord's clothing. (Gospel of St. John, chap. xix, v. 23. "The soldiers therefore, when they had crucified Him, took His garments and also His coat. Now the coat was without seam, woven from the top throughout.")

About ten feet further on, in the same direction, is a staircase of twenty-nine steps by which we descend to the

Chapel of St. Helena.

Here St. Helena sat while search was being made for the cross. From this chapel we descend a flight of thirteen steps into the Chapel of the Finding of the Cross, which belongs to the Franciscans. The Saviour being buried, all instruments used for the execution were, according to Jewish custom, buried. They were cast into an abandoned cistern, which was near the site of the crucifixion, and rubbish thrown over them. In the course of time, all kinds of offalls where thrown there so as to fill up the space.

In the year 326 St. Helena, after having destroyed the temples dedicated to idols, gave Calvary and the Holy Sepulchre to the veneration of the Christian world.

Chapel of the Finding of the Cross.

St. Helena consulted Bishop St. Macarius and the ancients of the city as to where she might find the august instrument of redemption. They pointed out the place to her, which she had carefully examined, and all the instruments of execution were found there as well as the crosses of the thieves; but no proofs were at hand to identify the cross which had borne the Saviour of mankind. The holy bishop therefore ordered public prayers to God, that He would deign to make it known. Then the bishop, accompanied by St. Helena, went to the house of a sick woman, known by mostly all the inhabitants to be in agony. After a short prayer, the holy bishop touched her with the three crosses; at the touch of the last cross, the woman was instantaneously cured. On the same day St. Macarius met a funeral procession going to the cemetery; he stopped those who carried the bier and touched the corpse with the crosses of the tnieves without result, but, upon touching the remains with the true cross, the dead person was suddenly restored to life.

In order to continue the excursion, we re-ascended the two staircases. Arriving on the nave we immediately saw a Greek chapel, in the center of which is an iron cage containing the pillar of opprobrium; a grayish granite pillar, which, according to tradition, served as a seat for Our Lord when crowned with thorns, abused and loaded with insult. It was brought from the praetorium of Pilate. (Gospel of St. Matth., chap. xxvii, v. 29: "And platting a crown of thorns, they put it upon his head.")

About thirty feet to the west, we passed by the staircase which leads by eighteen steps to Calvary. A door to the west below, leads into the

Chapel of Adam.

Upon entering, we saw to the right a stone slab which replaces the tomb of Godfrey de Bouillon, who conquered Jerusalem in the year 1099. At the extremity of the chapel of Adam, we see a small excavation, where, according to tradition, reposed the skull of the first man. Here to-day we can see the rent on the rock of Calvary. Ascending a flight of eighteen steps outside of the Chapel of Adam and the chamber of Godfrey, the low-vaulted chapel of Golgatha is entered.

Calvary.

At the east end is a platform about ten feet long, seven feet wide and twenty inches high. In the center is the Crucifixion Altar, belonging to the Schismatic Greeks; under the mensa or table, lying on the floor, is a marble slab with a hole in which our Saviour's cross was placed; to the left and right are seen the holes in which the crosses of the two thieves stood. In the marble pavement on the platform is another opening, through which is seen a rent in the rock, which is continuous with the one below in the Chapel of Adam. South of the altar, to the right is another division, called the Chapel of the Crucifixion. It was here that Christ was nailed to the cross. This part does not stand on the rock, but forms a kind of upper story, which is accounted for by the fact that St. Helena removed the ground beneath it and took it to Rome. On this altar I said Mass. Aside of this altar is another, indicating the spot where the Blessed Virgin Mary and St. John stood, watching the crucifixion. On Palm Sunday I said Mass on this altar.

On Wednesday in Holy Week, the pilgrims sang along in the Tenebræ, which was sung before the Holy Sepulchre. The Franciscan Fathers sang splendid and very impressive indeed; especially touching were the last words of each lamentation: "Jerusalem, Jerusalem, convert to the Lord, thy God!" While the Tenebræ was being sung, the master of ceremonies asked me to sing the VII. Lesson, which I did with great pleasure.

THE WAY OF THE CROSS AND PALM SUNDAY.

On Good Friday the pilgrims went the Way of the Cross, Via Dolorosa, which is in the streets of Jerusalem. At the buildings are marked the fourteen memorable events of our redemption. As many hundreds of people had joined us, the streets were totally blocked. At each station one of the Franciscan Fathers gave a little explanation or sermon. The last five stations are within the Holy Sepulchre Church.

On the evening of Holy Thursday we went the Way of the Cross inside the Holy Sepulchre Church, during which time eight sermons were held, each in a different language. Monsignor Setonpreached the English sermon, which was very eloquent and impressive, while the sermon on Mount Calvary was held in German.

The ceremony was especially touching on Calvary. On the spot where the crucifixion took place a subdeacon held a cross, on which was fixed a corpus. At the XIII station, where Christ is taken from the cross, a deacon took a pair of tongs, with which he extracted the nails from the hands, after which the arms hung down naturally; after loosening the feet he took the corpus down, laid it in a fine linen cloth, carried down from Calvary by four subdeacons, wearing very precious black dalmatics, and coming to the stone of unction they laid the corpus thereon. Then the Franciscan Guardian enbalmed it, as the body of Christ was embalmed according to the Jewish custom, and carried it into the Holy Sepulchre Chapel to represent burial. I never before saw such a touching and beautiful ceremony. The whole service lasted three hours. The church was crowded, there being about twenty thousand strangers in Jerusalem during Holy Week.

On Palm Sunday, at eight o'clock in the morning, the pilgrims went into Holy Sepulchre Church with the Latin patriarch, Monsignor Vincenzo Bracco (with whom we also had audience), who now blessed the palms before the Holy Sepulchre. Each of us pilgrims received one from him, after which we marched in procession around the Holy Sepulchre, through two rows of armed soldiers, who stood on guard. On the afternoon of Holy Thursday the Latin patriarch washed the feet of eight priests and four lay men. Of the priests of our pilgrimage who had this honor were Revs. J. M. Nardiello, J. C. Dunn and M. E. Kane.

THE GREEK FIRE ON HOLY SATURDAY.

On Holy Saturday we witnessed an interesting ceremony, called "the Greek Fire", performed in the Holy Sepulchre Church by the Schismatic Greeks. From Wednesday on in Holy Week, many hundreds of Schismatic Greeks rented a small space in the church, which they could occupy day and night (as they here slept on the floor every night) until Holy Saturday, when shortly before 12 o'clock noon, the patriarch of the Schismatic Greeks went into the chapel of the Holy Sepulchre. At 12 o'clock the signal was given by the large bell, whereupon the patriarch handed fire through one of the small apertures or windows of the chapel. They say and believe that this fire comes from heaven. Each one of the twenty or thirty thousand people who were within the Basilica, had a bundle of wax candles. Each person endeavored to get fire first from the patriarch, and as soon as received, ran through the crowd as speedy as possible. Others again tried to get fire from these and in the great confusion, would set fire to their clothes and even to their beards, thus causing the greatest excitement and confusion ever seen, despite the 800 soldiers who were present to maintain order. We saw many being knocked down and trampled upon by others, who were in haste of getting to their homes in Bethlehem, Jericho and Jaffa. After they got out of the crowd they put the fires in their lanterns. The fire was even taken on the steamer, sailing from Jaffa to Russia. They believe that if they reach their home with the fire they will surely go to heaven.

THE CŒNACULUM.

The Cœnaculum is on Mount Sion, within the city walls. It was in the Cœnaculum where Our Divine Saviour instituted the Blessed Sacrament. St. Luke, chap. xxii, v. 14: "And when the hour was come, He sat down and the twelve apostles with Him ......" V. 19: "And taking bread, He gave thanks and broke and gave to them, saying: 'This is my body which is given to you; do this for a commemoration of me.'" Here Our Divine Saviour washed the feet of His apostles, promised them the Holy Ghost and foretold the treason and the denial of St. Peter. Here Jesus appeared twice to His disciples; first, on the day of His resurrection, and again eight days later when He made St. Thomas touch with his finger His sacred wounds. Here the Holy Ghost descended upon the apostles and the Sacrament of Confirmation was instituted. Here St. Paula venerated the pillar at which Our Lord had been scourged, and which, as she said, was still stained by this precious blood. According to St. Ephiphanius, the Cœnaculum was not destroyed by Titus. He tells us in his "Book of Mensurus", cited by Anaresmius, that Adrian, coming from Egypt, found Jerusalem destroyed to the ground, except some few houses near the Cœnaculum, then converted into a church.

In the beginning of the fourteenth century, St. Helena built a beautiful church over the Cœnaculum. Although it has often been destroyed and rebuilt, it always consisted, as now, of two stories. The first story was for a long period the harem or dwelling of the wives of Mussulmen of the province of Nabi Daoud.

In 1244, Sultan Salahad, a friend to St. Francis de Assissi gave the Franciscans a hospital, situated near the Cœnaculum. Some time after, the sultan of Egypt declared war against his uncle and conquered him, whereafter all the Christians were banished. After a persecution of short duration the Franciscans reestablished themselves on Mount Sion. At the request of F. Ruggers Guarini, Robert of Anjou, king of Sicily, and Sancha, his wife, purchased the Cœnaculum from the sultan and gave it to the Holy See, upon the condition that the Franciscans should be the perpetual guardians thereof. This was granted in a bull of Pope Clement VI., beginning thus: "*Nuper carissimi in Christo,*" given at Avignon, November 21, 1342. And another begins: *Gratias agaomnium bonorum largiri etc.*" It was then that the Franciscans built the church which now exists. It is small, and constructed of material, taken from the churches which preceded it, as can principally be seen on the pillars, supporting the ceiling and the arch; one is of granite; the other a stone of the country. The smaller pillars are also of various sizes and different kinds of stone.

In 1335, a rich lady named Sophis, of Florence, wishing to provide for the wants of the sick and the pilgrims, bought the ground surrounding the convent and built the great establishment, placed by Innocent IV. under the care of the Franciscan Fathers, who exercised hospitality here for two centuries, notwithstanding the continual vexations from the Turks and the incursions of the Arabs, which cost the lives of over two-hundred religious. The Mussulmen ceased not to seek every possible means of expelling the Christians from this place, especially since the time that the rumor was spread, that the tomb of David was within one of the ground floor habitations. They pretended to honor according to their own fashion the sepulchre of the king-prophet, and managed to usurp the guardianship thereof in 1555. Once within the ground they made rapid progress. In 1550, almost all the Franciscans were massacred and the church converted into a mosque named "Nabi Daoud (Prophet David)". It is a mosque to this day and still bears the same name.

As for the tomb of David, Scripture says: "David was buried on Mount Sion. There exists great doubt that it was on this spot. The Mussulmen show a block of masonry, very modern in its details, covered with a green table cover. If anyone tells them that this cannot be the real tomb, they reply that the true tomb of David is in a vault beneath the mausoleum, where, out of respect, no man can enter.

As we pilgrims came out of the Cœnaculum, Mr. John Manning one of our pilgrims was about to take our photographs in a group, but as soon as the Mussulmen saw that, they chased him away and followed us for quite a while, scolding the whole time.

TOMB OF THE BLESSED VIRGIN.

The pilgrims also visited this holy tomb. A flight of 48 steps leads to the Church of the Assumption. Having reached the twenty-first step on the right hand at the main wall of the building, a small chapel with two altars, touching each other, is seen. According to tradition, the first on the left side, or to the north upon entering, is over the tomb of St. Joachim and the other opposite, over that of St. Anna. At the foot of the steps we see to the west a cistern and near by, an altar belonging to the Schismatic Copts.

Near by at the foot of Mt. Sion is the

GROTTO OF THE AGONY.

To this grotto, where our Divine Lord, on the eve of His passion, perspired blood, the pilgrims went next. St. Luke, chap. xxii, v. 39; "And going out He went according to his custom to the mount of Olives; and His disciples also followed Him......" V. 44: "And His sweat became as drops of blood, trickling down upon the ground." We decend therein by a flight of six steps.

It is a natural grotto or cave, lighted by an opening through the top. It contains three altars. The exact spot of the agony is shown under the main altar and below on the floor is a tin star on which the following words can be read: "Hic Jesus sanguinem sudavit." I said mass in this grotto.

Since 1392, the Franciscan Fathers of the Holy Land say three masses here daily. Near this grotto is the place, which was shown to us, where the apostles slept whilst Christ was praying in the grotto. Right aside of this grotto is the Garden of Gethsemane in which the Franciscan Fathers have many beautiful flowers of which each one of us received some. In this garden are also some very old and large olive trees. If these are not the same trees, they nevertheless sprung from the roots of those trees, which shaded many times the Man-God and were witnesses of His sighs and the flames of love issuing from His over-adorable heart and ascending to His Eternal Father.

MOUNT OLIVES.

This mountain lies east of Jerusalem. At present there are still many olive trees along this mount. Three roads lead to this celebrated mountain, so often mentioned in both the old and new testament. The first road commences at the gate at the Garden of Gethsemane and passes around the so-called "Tomb of the Prophets." The other roads begin at the northeast angle of said garden. The one ascending the steepest side passes by the spot where Jesus wept over the ungrateful city. Here I read to our pilgrims the gospel, which speaks of Christ, weeping over Jerusalem. Near by, we see a rock where according to ancient tradition, St. Thomas, being on his way to visit the grave of the Blessed

Virgin, saw her ascending to heaven, she letting her girdle fall to him on this same rock. The Greeks especially have a great veneration for this rock.

On the summit of Mount Olives we saw the spot from where Christ ascended into heaven.

THE VALLEY OF JOSEPHAT.

At the base of Mount Olives and to the west is the Valley of Josephat, where, according to the prophet Joel (chap. iii. "The Lord shall judge all nations in the valley of Josephat......") the final judgment will take place.

The valley of Josephat, furrowed by the torrent Cedron, has a width of about 400 feet. It begins adjacent to the tomb of the judges, northwest of Jerusalem being narrower below Gethsemane, where it joins the Valley of the sons of Hennon, southeast. Here it is only as broad as the Cedron and is called valley of fire (on a di en Nar). Its length is about three Kilometers (3000 feet).

THE MOSQUE OF OMAR.

This mosque, which the pilgrims also visited, is considered by the Mussulmen one of their principal sanctuaries. It is also called Koubletes-Sakhrah, (cupola of the rock). It has an octagonal front, each division being encased in marble and squares of porcelain, coarsely varnished. Sixty feet from the front are seven windows of colored glass. The mosque is crowned by a cupola, covered with copper and surmounted by a large crescent. Towards each of the cardinal points is a door. The door through which we entered is styled "Gate of David."

Formerly, the Christians who dared to pass only the surrounding wall, were punished with death. Since the last war in the East, the mosque has become accessible to Europeans, having a permit from their respecive consuls, from the governor of Jerusalem. Nevertheless, it is closed to visitors during the days of the great Mussulman Lent, called Ramadan, and on all Fridays in the year.

Before entering, each person must pay a fee of five francs (about one dollar) and put on a pair of slippers.

The interior is dark, two concentrical octagonal divisions surrounding the central part. The first is formed by the exterior wall and the second by eight pillars and sixteen columns of beautiful marble, the base of which is one piece. All upper parts of the mosque are covered by mosaics and rich gilding, interspersed with text from the Koran, in gilt letters. The central part is enclosed by four pillars and two columns of the same design as the foregoing. A handsome iron railing fills up the spaces between the columns. Besides this railing, we find another, artistically carved in wood, which surrounds the Sakhrah or Rock, which on this side is thirty feet wide, contrasting singularly with the rich ornamentation of the mosque. The surface of the Sakhrah is devoid of ornaments. Uneven, and a round hole having been bored into it perpendicularly, it is flat on the north and west sides. About five feet above it is suspended a Klemeh (kind of tent) made of red and green silk, which is to remind the believers of Mohammed of the tent given by God to Adam, who, having sought Eve for 100 years, found her on a mountain near Mecca.

This Sakhrah or Rock is venerable to both Christians and Jews, and to the Mussulmen it is actually as precious as was Ornam, which David purchased from the Jebuseens. It was honored by the fire from heaven which descended to consume the sacrifice offered by the king-prophet to the Lord; it was covered by the celebrated Temple of Solomon. The Ark of the Covenant was placed on this rock and this place was called Holy of Holies. The high-priest only had access to it, and that only once a year.

The Temple of Solomon was destroyed by Nabuchodonosor, and the Holy of Holies remained buried beneath its ruins. When the Jews returned from captivity Zerobabel rebuilt it, but the Holy of Holies remained empty, for, before the destruction of the temple, the Prophet Jeremiah had saved the Tabernacle, the Ark of the Covenant and the Altar of Incensing. Titus destroyed this temple and Adrian built one in its stead in honor of Jupiter.

Omar covered the rock with a mosque. The crusaders substituted the cross for the crescent, but when Saladin took the Holy City this emblem of our faith was definitely overthrown, the rock was washed with rose-water and the place became again a Mohammedan sanctuary.

At the western extremity of the rock we see what looks like an impression from a hand; this is attributed to the Archangel Gabriel. With this is connected a legend. Mohammed, being mounted on El-Borak, the white horse, which was a present from the archangel set out for heaven to arrange their important affairs; but the rock (or Sakhrah) arose so as to follow the prophet. God, not wishing to deprive the world of this rock, sent the Archangel Gabriel who with his hand restrained the movements, leaving the impression of his hand thereon. To the southwest angle of the Sakhrah is a sort of a cage, made of iron, in which there is a piece of marble. We are allowed to pass our hand through a small opening and touch the print of Mohammed's foot, which he left on this marble.

At the southern door of the mosque a copy of the Koran is shown, said to have belonged to the Caliph Omar.

PLACE WHERE THE JEWS GO TO WEEP.

On Mount Sion, near the Mosque of Omar, is an old wall, said to be a remnant of the old temple of the Jews. To this wall the Jews—men, women and children—go every Friday afternoon to sigh, lament, pray and weep over the destruction of their renowned temple. We went to see them weep on a Friday. It is a touching and pitiful sight. The following are the two principal prayers which they recite or sing in choir:

Rabbi—On account of the palace which is devastated,

People—We sit solitary whilst we weep.

R.—On account of our walls which are cast down,

P.—We sit solitary whilst we weep.

R.—On account of our glory which we passed,

P.—We sit solitary whilst we weep.

R.—On account of our great men, now no more,

P.—We sit solitary whilst we weep.

R.—On account of our precious stones which are buried.

P.—We sit solitary whilst we weep.

R.—On account of our priests who have stumbled,

P.—We sit solitary whilst we weep.

R.—On account of our kings who have despised them,

P.—We sit solitary whilst we weep.

Rabbi—We beseech Thee to have pity on Sion,
People—Reassemble the children of Jerusalem.
R.—Hasten, hasten, O Saviour of Sion,
P.—Speak in favor of Jerusalem.
R.—That beauty and majesty may surround Sion,
P.—Turn with clemency towards Jerusalem.
R.—That the royal power may soon be reestablished in Sion,
P.—Comfort these who weep over Jerusalem.
R.—That peace and happiness may enter Sion,
P.—And the rod of Thy power be raised over Jerusalem.

Here we can principally see the verification of the words of the Prophet Jeremiah, saying to this stubborn people: "Why weep you because ye are beaten with rods? Your sorrow is incurable. On acccunt of the multitude of your sins I have treated you thus." It is truly a sad spectacle to see these people dispersed and wandering all over the world, come to Jerusalem, there to live and die, when it was their forefathers who were guilty of the fearful crime of killing their God, and who uttered this prophetic cry: "Let His blood be upon us!" This unhappy nation is a terrible and permanent proof of the oracles, pronounced by the prophets and evangelists. So is it heartrending to see them weep in that land where they crucified Him who came to deliver them.

Formerly this nation wept and prayed on the site of their ancient temple, but since the Mosque of Omar was built they are forced to be satisfied with being allowed to do so within an enclosure on a flagged spot and that at a distance. At sunset they all leave the place. Thus they have wept since the coming of Christ, and thus they will weep every Friday as long as this world will exist. The Messiah has come, and as man He will come no more. They expect the Messiah to come to-day or to-morrow and rebuild their temple.

TRIP FROM JERUSALEM TO JERICHO.

During our sojourn in the Holy City, the second and third sections of our pilgrims made a trip on horse-back to Jericho, the first section going to Bethlehem in the meantime. We could not be at Jericho at one time, as the accomodation there for so many was very poor. After our return, we, the second and third section, went to Bethlehem and the other section to Jericho. When we told them of the horrible and dangerous road and of the hard times we had had, many of them did not go.

Early in the morning of the 10th of April we went to the Jaffa Gate, where our guides awaited us with Arabian horses, ready to mount. These horses are of medium size and very hardy. They run for miles in that hot country, in the greatest heat, without getting one wet hair. If the sadles were as good as the horses, riding would be easier. On horse-back is the only means of going to Jericho, as the path, or road, if we can call it such, is at some places very narrow, rough and stony, and the entire length of it twists around in the mountain ravines, that at times one can hardly see the road for more than a distance of twenty or thirty steps ahead. On each side are high, rocky mountains which makes travel by vehicles impossible. Along these fearful ravines we met, time and again, fierce-looking and well armed Bedouins, so that we were involuntarily reminded of the gospel which reads: "A man went from Jerusalem to Jericho and fell among robbers, who stripped and wounded him." This very gospel was verified on one of our pilgrims. About one hour after our departure from Jerusalem, one of our pilgrims was thrown from his horse and severely hurt; so our guides told two Arabians to take the wounded man, bring him to Jerusalem and place him in a hospital. Our guides thought they were good Samaritans, who would take care of the man; but the trouble was that they were only too good, as they even took care of his watch and money. (St. Luke, chap. x, v. 30, 33 and 34.) "A certain man went from Jerusalem to Jericho and fell amongst robbers; but a good Samaritan being on his journey, came near him, and, seeing him, was moved with compassion, and, going up to him, bound up his wounds, pouring in oil and wine, and setting him upon his own beast, brought him to an inn and took care of him."

On our way we took dinner which our guides had taken along from Jerusalem, in this very inn. According to tradition this is the same inn referred to in the gospel, and it is probable, since along the whole distance there is no other house and this one is very old and just suitable for travelers. It is a very old and delapidated one-story stone structure and has a large porch to it in the rear. The whole back ground is enclosed by a massive stone wall, where travelers tie their horses, donkeys or camels.

We rested here about two hours, and at two o'clock rode on again towards Jericho. Along the road we met more "Good Samaritans," inhabitants of the country, who would stop some of our party every once in a while, loosen a buckle on either bridle or saddle and say that it was torn, although there was nothing the matter. Of course this was a new way of getting "bakchiche." This is somewhat similar to what one of our reverend pilgrims told me. When about to leave Naples, an Italian had shaken hands with him and wished him a good journey; for this service the Italian had asked one franc. The priest gave it to the fellow, as he would not have got rid of him otherwise.

At last, being very tired and worn out by fatigue and heat, we arrived at Jericho about six o'clock that evening. There we all stopped at a small hotel. Some were obliged to sleep under tents, which were just as good, as these tents, which we had used in the Holy Land for over three weeks, were as good and convenient as could be. About nine o'clock in the evening some thirty Bedouins from the neighborhood came in front of our hotel. They sang and danced, which was very amusing to us, but, of course, we had to pay two francs each "bakchiche."

Jericho, once a flourishing city of Palestine, near the Dead Sea, in the valley of the Jordan, now has only about seven houses. It was at one time one of the richest cities of Canaan, beautifully situated and encircled by groves of balsam and palm trees. Jericho was the first city Josue took from the Canaanites; at the sound of the trumpets he overthrew its walls and put to the sword all its inhabitants except one woman named Rahab; she and her family were spared on account of the protection which she offered to spies of Josue, who had come to view the country. (Josue, chap. vi, v. 22: "But Josue said to two men who had been sent out as spies: 'Go into the harlot's house and bring her out and all things that are hers.'" V. 23: "And the young men went in and brought out Rahab." V. 24: "But they burnt the city and all things that were therein") Josue uttered this curse against Jericho: V. 26. "Cursed be the man before the Lord that shall raise up and build the city of Jericho; in his first-born may he lay the foundation thereof, and in the last of his children set up its gates!"

During the reign of Achab, Hiel of Bethel undertook to rebuild Jericho, and by it experienced the terrible curse, for he lost his oldest son, Abiram, while yet laying the foundations: the last of his sons, Segub, died when erecting the gates. (III Kings, chap. xvi, v. 34.)

At daybreak of the next day we again mounted our horses and started towards the Dead Sea. After we had left Jericho, we passed several tents of Bedouins, who with torches carried fire from one tent to another. Around Jericho there is abundant water flowing from the Fountain of Eliseus, and the valley is also fertile. But the farmer is unable to get what he sows on account of the Bedouins and other robbers, consequently the environs of Jericho are full of briars and thorny trees. After riding about two hours we came to the

DEAD SEA.

This sea lies eighteen miles east of Jerusalem, between two immense chains of mountains, the Moab Mountains to the east and the Hebron Mountains to the west. In the Mountains of Moab and north of the Dead Sea is Nebo, where Moses died in sight of the promised land. (1451 B. C.) (Deuteronomy, chap. xxxiv, v. 5: "And Moses, the servant of the Lord, died there, in the land of Moab, by the commandment of the Lord." V. 1: "Then Moses went up from the Plains of Moab upon Mount Nebo.")

The Dead Sea is about forty miles long from north to south. Where this water is once stood the cities of Sodom and Gomorrah. According to Lieut. Lynch and others its depth is 1,300 feet. Its water is bitter, salty and very disagreeable to the taste. We tasted it. When put into a tumbler it is as clear as any other water. Bodies, when thrown in, float on it with greater buoyancy than in any other sea. When something is dipped in and taken out, the water evaporates immediately, leaving a salt crust. About five of our party bathed in it, and they said, that as soon as they came into it three or four feet deep they were lifted up and that it is almost impossible to drown. We remained here about one-half hour then rode to the River Jordan.

THE JORDAN.

We arrived here after one hour's ride. Before we arrived our guides had erected a tent on the shore, in which Rt. Rev. Bishop Rademacher, Very Rev. Chas. Vissani and another priest said Masses on portable altars. The Jordan empties into the Dead Sea. It has its source from the Libanus. It enters the sea of Genesareth. Some of the pilgrims bathed in it. Our guides showed them some safe places. One must keep near the shore so as to avoid the strong current. In some places we noticed the water going down on one side of the shore and the opposite shore it flowed up. It inclines a great deal; hence the rapidity of its waters. The entire length of the Jordan is about 120 miles, and its width from eighty to ninety feet. Considerable cane grows along the shores, and the surrounding country is the Eden of Palestine.

About two o'clock in the afternoon some of us mounted our horses to start back for Jericho, but our guides called us back, saying that it was not advisable for us, as the heat was very intense.

It was about four o'clock when we all started back for Jericho, where we arrived at about six o'clock. We stopped a while and refreshed ourselves somewhat. Afterwards we rode to the fountain of Eliseus, located about twenty-five minutes from Jericho. It is named after the prophet, because its water could not be used and he made it wholesome. After we arrived there we all drank of it.

The inhabitants of Jericho complained to the prophet that the water was not potable; he then told them to bring a new pitcher and some salt. (IV. Kings, chap. ii, v. 19: "And the men of the city said to Eliseus: 'Behold, the situation of this city is very good, as thou, our lord, seest, but the waters are very bad and the ground barren.'" V. 20: "And he said: 'Bring me a new vessel and put salt into it.'" V. 21: "And when they had brought it, he went out to the spring of the waters, cast the salt into it and said: 'Thus sayeth the Lord: I have healed these waters, and there shall be no more in them death or barrenness." V. 22: "And the waters were healed until this day, according to the words of Eliseus, which he spoke.")

THE QUARANTINE MOUNTAIN.

Having stopped at the fountain for about fifteen minutes, the pilgrims returned to Jericho for supper, whilst Rev. George Meyer, Mr. John Hoebing, Brother Bernardin and myself went to the Quarantine Mountain, which we reached in about twenty minutes. This mountain is thus named, because Our

Lord fasted there forty days and forty nights, after which He was tempted by the devil on the top of the same mountain; consequently it is also called Mount of Temptation.

This mountain is entirely perforated with cells, which in former times were inhabited by Anchorites. Many of these cells are natural cavities, while some have been dug out. The one lying near the western angle of the mountain has an ogival entrance, and is, according to tradition, the same one in which Our Lord dwelt during the days of His fasting. Near it is a kind of a narrow stone path, which we ascended with our horses as far as they could go. Just then we met a Turk coming down, whom we paid a few francs to hold our horses until we came down. Then we walked up on a stone steps about one hundred feet high, until we were finally in the cave. The ascent was very tiresome. The cave is about forty feet long. At one end of it live three Schismatic Greeks, who have a small convent in the cave. They received their ammunition from Jerusalem. They received us kindly and treated us to a little glassful of excellent brandy. After we had been through the cave we returned to Jericho and took supper. The next morning we made an early start for Jerusalem. About nine o'clock A. M. we came to that inn, took lunch, and arrived at Bethania about twelve o'clock noon.

BETHANIA.

Bethania is at present a dirty hamlet of about twenty families. It lies three miles from Jerusalem on the east slope of Mount Olives. Bethania is mentioned in the New Testament as the place where Christ lodged, where He was anointed and where He raised Lazarus from the dead. There are still some ruins, which were pointed out to us, where the house of Mary and Martha should have stood. Bethania is especially known for the tomb of Lazarus, which is a deep vault in the lime-stone rock. We entered it by a little door opening to the north, and by a flight of twenty-seven steps, made by the Franciscan Fathers. From the vestibule we descended three steps and then entered a low and difficult passage which leads to the tomb of Lazarus. (Gospel St. John, chap. xi, v. 1: "Now there was a certain man sick, named Lazarus, of Bethania, of the town of Mary, and Martha her sister.") The

Franciscan Fathers come here several times in a year to offer the Holy Sacrifice. About two o'clock in the afternoon we were in Jerusalem again, entirely worn out.

BETHLEHEM.

Sunday afternoon, April 14th, the second and third section rode on wagons to Bethlehem, which is six miles south of Jerusalem. Upon our arrival, we went to the convent of the Franciscan Fathers, where we were received very kindly. As we could not go to the Grotto of the Nativity immediately, we refreshed ourselves somewhat, and went directly to the Grotto of the Shepherds, about twenty-five minutes' walk east of Bethlehem. In going there we descended from Bethlehem and passed by the village of the shepherds. Here lives a Schismatic Greek priest, who has the key of the Grotto. Bro. Bernardin sent him word. After we went on a piece, the Greek passed us with the key, accompanied by a boy, who, as Bro. Bernardin told us, was the son of the Greek monk. After proceeding for about fifteen minutes, we came to the Grotto of the Shepherds. It is situated in the centre of a square, planted with olive trees and surrounded by a delapidated wall of dry stones. The Franciscan Fathers planted most of these olive trees when the grotto was still in their possession. The Greeks have been in possession of it since the year 1818.

This chapel, which is in a little stone building, called the Grotto of the Shepherds, is, according to tradition, the ancient crypt of the church built by St. Helena, over the place where the angel of the Lord announced to the shepherds the birth of Christ. I read to the pilgrims in the Chapel of the Shepherds the Gospel of St. Luke, chap. ii, from the eighth verse, which says: "And there were in the same country shepherds watching and keeping the night watches over their flock." V. 9: "And behold an angel of the Lord stood by them, and the brightness of God shone round about them, and they feared with a great fear, etc.," till verse 21.

Returning, we immediately went into the church of St. Catharine, of the Franciscan Convent. After supper a procession was formed, and amid singing of hymns, we solemnly entered the Grotto of the Nativity by a flight of sixteen steps. Having entered the Holy Grotto, we find on the eastern side a semi-circular apse (a kind of a little altar), which encloses the precise spot of the birth of Christ. On this principal altar we Latins can not say Mass, as the Schismatic Greeks, who took possession of it, will not allow us. Here Very Rev. Chas. Vissani addressed the pilgrims in a few but touching words. This place still preserves some remains of the beautiful painting in mosaics, representing the new born Saviour. Around the apse and near to the ground, burn day and night fifteen lamps; of these, four belong to the Latins, five to the Armenians and six to the Schismatic Greeks. A slab of white marble which covers the ground floor of the apse, shows through an aperture in its center a blueish colored stone, like of jaspar; the aperture has a silver star, bearing around it this inscription: *"Hic de Virgine Maria Jesus Christus natus est.* Here Jesus Christ was born of the Virgin Mary." In this apse is a table, which serves as an altar for the Greeks and Armenians, to celebrate the Holy Sacrifice. Right opposite this apse, about nine feet south-west, we descend by three steps into the oratory of the manger, which is six feet long and six feet wide. It is hewed out in the rock. The north and north-eastern sides, which are open, are supported by three marble pillars. To the east, within this oratory is an altar dedicated to the Three Holy Kings, erected over the spot where they adored Christ and offered their gifts. This altar still belongs to the Latins. The Holy Grotto or Subterranean Chapel of the Nativity is thirty feet long, twelve feet wide and a little over seven feet high, and is paved with large flags of white marble. The sides of the rock, which serve as walls are covered with similar slabs. The upper part and the sides otherwise seem natural, neither frescoed nor white-washed. Thirty-one lamps, seven belonging to the Latins, burn constantly in this venerable grotto. There are also other caves alongside of the Grotto of Nativity, which are connected with it by narrow passages. Here is erected the Chapel of St. Joseph, from which we descend by five steps into another chapel, dedicated to the Holy Innocents. In one of the caves is also a chapel dedicated to St. Jerome, and has also an altar over his tomb. According to tradition, it was here that the Saint passed his nights and days in study and prayer. On the porch of the Basilica we saw a door giving access to the Armenian Convent (Schismatic), where a hall is shown called the School of St. Jerome, because in it the Saint taught publicly the Christian Doctrine. A large church is built over the Grotto of the Nativity. At two o'clock the next morning we started to say Mass in the Holy Grotto.

Grotto of the Milk.

The next morning after we had said Mass and taken breakfast, we went from the Franciscan Convent to the Grotto of Milk, about ten minutes' walk. Tradition tells us that St. Joseph, having been informed by the angel, that Herod sought the Divine Jesus, took the Holy Virgin and her child for refuge to this grotto, to wait for a more favorable moment to continue their flight. The Blessed Mother there nursed her Jesus; some drops of her virginal milk, falling to the ground, have given to this site the virtue of procuring for all nurses in want of it, a supply. Whether Catholics, Schismatics or even Turks, all have recourse in this necessity to the grotto. They take some of the stone, which is chalky and easily dissolved, put it into a little water or other liquid and drink it. After having besought the intercession of the Blessed Virgin, many have obtained the desired favor. In the grotto a Franciscan Father gave each one of us two or three of these stones. Here, at Bethlehem, we were all very jolly; it was strange, and when Father Vissani asked the Superior of the Franciscans how that was, he replied: "Bethlehem is a place of continual joy. Those Franciscan Fathers deserve all credit and support, as they even give their lives. Thousands of them were killed already in Palestine; 4,000, in order to preserve the Holy Places."

In the afternoon, at two o'clock some of our pilgrims went to St. John in the Mountain, and others returned to Jerusalem. Bethlehem has about 4,000 inhabitants.

FEW REMARKS ABOUT THE PRESENT JERUSALEM.

For the Mohammedans, Jerusalem ranks next in sanctity to Mecca and Medina, and is the Holy City for Jews and Christians likewise. The country around Jerusalem is rocky; the crops are not much as the soil is not fertile. The ground in many parts is covered with large stones and has a sad and barren appearance. The city is built very irregular. It has at present five open gates:

The Jaffa Gate on the west (this is the principal one); the Damascus Gate on the north; St. Stephen's Gate on the east; the Zion Gate on the south; the other is called Dung Gate.

The gate through which Our Lord on Palm Sunday triumphantly entered Jerusalem, called the Golden gate, is at present walled up. Here a Mohammedan soldier stands continually on guard, for the Turks believe, that through this gate the Christians will one day come and take possession of the city. Its streets are uneven, poorly paved, narrow, winding and very dirty. Some streets are only four to six feet wide. All this accounts for it that we see no vehicle whatever in the streets of Jerusalem. All building materials, such as stone, timber, etc., are transported on donkeys and camels. We sometimes saw as many as fifteen or twenty camels, one behind the other, a regular procession, all loaded with large timber, fifteen or twenty feet long, fastened one on each side of the shoulder, the one end dragging on the ground. Time and again we saw these poor animals break down under the heavy weight. As we could not pass, we had a good chance to observe the whole proceedings. When a camel is about to be loaded, he lays down, and when loaded gets up himself. It is an interesting sight. Ruble is put in baskets, and two hung on each donkey.

The houses are built of heavy masonry, with arched roofs, which are supported by thick walls. There is not much style about them, but as a general thing the rooms are well ventilated and lofty. The fronts are plain. The houses are usually two stories high. Few or no windows are seen in the first stories. The doors are so low that we must stoop when entering. The roofs rise in domes. The rooms receive light from interior courts, which, of course, in large houses forms an agreeable promenade. Sometimes they are constructed in gardens, where the families spend their leisure hours. They generally live in the upper stories, as in the first story they have their lumber, kitchen, stable, cistern, workshops and offices. Some are three or four hundred years old.

OUR CERTIFICATE OF JERUSALEM.

During our stay in the Holy City each pilgrim received the following certificate, stamped with the seal of the Custody of the Holy Land.

IN THE NAME OF GOD, AMEN.

ST. SAVIOUR'S CONVENT, JERUSALEM.

We, the Custos of the Holy Land, attest and declare to all those who read these presents, that REV. JAMES PFEIFFER, a pilgrim, happily reached Jerusalem on the 7th day of April, 1889; that on the following days he visited the principal Sanctuaries, in which the Saviour of the world mercifully delivered His beloved people and indeed, the lost millitude of the whole human race from the servitude of hell—namely Calvary—where Christ was crucified and, overcoming death, opened to us the doors of Heaven; the Holy Sepulchre, where His most sacred body was laid and rested for three days before His glorious Resurrection, and finally all those Sacred Places of Palestine, hallowed by the steps of Our Lord and His Blessed Mother, Mary; places usually visited by our religious and by pilgrims—and that said pilgrim celebrated the Holy Sacrifice of the Mass in these places.

In witness whereof we have granted this certificate through our Secretary, and sealed with our official seal.

Given at Jerusalem in our venerable Convent of the Holy Saviour, this 22d day of April, 1889.

FR. JOSEPH FROM ROME, O. S. F.,
Secretary of the Custody.

BETHEL.

On Easter Monday the second and third sections took leave of the first section, the latter leaving Jerusalem the next day, going back to Jaffa and then home, whilst the others began their big horse-back trip for Nazareth, up to

Beyrout. At an early hour on the day stated above, we went to the Jaffa Gate, where our guides had the horses ready for us. Each one could pick his own horse; whosoever came first had first choice.

After we had left the Jaffa Gate we directed our course northward, leaving on the left the road to St. John in the Mountains, and a little further on that of Jaffa. After we had gone on about twenty minutes we came to Mount Sekopus. Here, on this height, we all stopped, taking a good and last view of the Holy City. Saluting it, we continued our difficult journey until Bethel, which we reached about twelve o'clock noon. Here we stopped and ate dinner under our tent, pitched by our guides. To-day there are nothing but ruins at Bethel. It is about eleven miles north of Jerusalem. Here Jacob beheld in a vision the angels ascend and descend. Here Abraham separated from his nephew Lot, on account of the disputes of their shepherds (1,933 years before Christ). Jacob flying from the wrath of his brother Esau passed the night here. Jacob, on his return from Mesopotamia built here an altar to Jehovah. The Prophet Amos prophesied against Bethel, saying: "Seek not Bethel; Go not to Galgala; pass not to Bersaber, because Galgala shall be led captive and Bethel shall be reduced to nothing." (Amos, chap. v.)

On leaving Bethel at three o'clock P. M., we left the Tribe of Benjamin to enter that of Ephraim. We directed our course north, until about two hours afterward, when we came into the beautiful Valley of Jifna. Here at Jifna, a little village of about 300 inhabitants, half of whom are Catholics, the rest Schismatic Greeks, we pitched our tents for the night. Tuesday morning, April 23d, about six o'clock, we left and ascended the Ridge of Shiloh, from where we rode over the hills and valleys to the Plain of Mukhna; then rode up the valley to Jacob's Well and Joseph's Tomb. From the tomb we went up the valley between Mount Gerizim and Ebal (or Mount Gerisim), down past the end of Naplous, to our tents, which were here pitched, north of the town on a piece of ground rented for this purpose. Naplous is the site of ancient Sychar or Shichem. It was a city of refuge.

NAPLOUS.

This town is situated about thirty miles north of Jerusalem and has 20,000 inhabitants, about 100 of whom are Catholics; 500, Schismatic Greeks; 240, Samaritans, about the same number of Jews, and the balance are Mohammedans. It has a Latin Missionary. The city is long, the streets are dark and narrow, most of them being arched over, and the pavements are very slippery. Most of its little commerce is in soap and cotton. The only interesting object for us at Naplous was the Pentateuch, written in the Samaritan Language and with Samaritan letters, on large sheets of parchment, rolled round small wands. This precious manuscript is kept in the Samaritan Synagogue, where we paid four or five piasters to see it.

The City of Naplous is pleasantly situated in a beautiful and fertile valley, between the Mountains of Hebal and Garizim; it is watered by several excellent streams. Here, at Naplous, we had our tents pitched near a Turkish cemetery. Near it, under a small building, supported by four stone columns, sides open, were some thirty women and a few small boys, screaming and weeping. They were weeping women of whom the Gospel speaks. Rev. Christopher Hughes was the first one who noticed these; so he went there, and after he was fooled he came back and told Mr. John Hoebing to go up there as there were some women crying; it seemed to him they had a dead person lying there; but, said he, you must go up very close to see it well. So John Hoebing came and told me about it, and I told Rev. George Meyer, after which we started on, going pretty fast, for fear it might be all over by the time we got there. When we came somewhat near, we saw they were kneeling and sitting on the ground, clapping their hands, lamenting and weeping for all that was in them; but we could see nothing else. As I was ahead of my two companions I tried to get as close to the weeping women and children as possible, as Rev. Hughes had told us; but as soon as we attempted to go near them, they came towards us shaking their fists, and the little boys picked up stones. Now, since Father Meyer had a kind of a white bed-sheet hanging over him, on account of the great heat, I told him to go up closer, because his costume was somewhat similar to the kind they wore, and they might think him one of them (always thinking go up very close); so he made attempts to get closer, courageous as he always was, and began to salute them in their language, saying: "*Salem alei Rum*. Peace be with you;" but they responded his well meant salutation by nearly rushing on to us and hurling stones at us. Then they called a policeman who stood on guard not very far off. As soon as I noticed that I retraced. Father Meyer was not in a great hurry, so the policeman gave him to understand that he had to go away. Father Meyer, still not in a great hurry, (I suppose because he saluted them so nicely, and meant it so well), the policeman gave him a push; then I told him to come along, or he might get into trouble; so we had to go back without seeing what they had. Father Hughes in the meantime kept watching us, and if ever any man laughed hearty it was Father Hughes when we came back. A short while after we saw them carry a corpse out of the town to the grave-yard. We heard them weep during the whole night. Our guide afterwards told us that they weep thus for eight days; of course they were paid.

Early next morning we left Naplous, and rode down a fertile and well cultivated valley towards Samaria. We rode along the plateau, on which stood Ahab's ivory palace, and passed along the remains of a colonnade, which stood since the time of Herod. Along here we had a beautiful, wide pike. So Rev. M. J. Phelan, Mr. Frank Headon, Mr. Jos. Ismay and myself left the company and rode ahead. Father Phelan and myself often done so, because it was dangerous to remain in the crowd, which numbered over 100 horses. Our guides always wanted us to keep together as close as possible, which was, as I said before, very dangerous, for as soon as the horses came near to each other, they would begin to kick; in fact, that same afternoon a priest of our party was kicked by a horse and had a leg broken a few miles this side of Nazareth. He was carried in a kind of baldachin to the hospital in Nazareth, where he had to remain for three months. When we were about to leave our party, Mr. Giled, our guide, advised us to remain in the company, as he would not send after us if we got lost. We went on nevertheless, thinking, that we would be able to see where the road turned off. As this was the only road, we kept on riding pretty fast, until we came to a little branch. Here we rested a short while, lit our pipes and left our horses drink. After we had been here a little while, I said to Father Phelan: "Why, it seems our folk are not coming!" "Oh yes" said he, "they are far behind; they are coming!" After having waited yet a while, I said, that it seemed they were not coming; that better some one take the best horse and ride back to see. "No," said Father Phelan, "we will all ride back." So we galloped back for about two miles. On the way we met an old raggy Arab, whom Father Phelan asked: "Did you see Cookey?" (Cookey, since we traveled under Cooks' guidance.) The Arab did not make a motion; so we on back, and at last we saw, on a hill to our left, persons riding. We felt relieved, thinking, that they were of our party; but as we came nearer, we saw that we had been mistaken. We then asked them, whether they had seen any of Cooks' party, which they answered in the negative. (These people were from England.) We rode on again and at last one of Cooks' guides came along, hunting us. As good luck would have, we were then on the right road, and not very far from Samaria, where our party was. They had turned off from the main road by a little path, which we had not noticed. We met our pilgrims again at Samaria.

In Samaria there are only few houses. There was shown to us a grave, said to be that of St. John the Baptist.

After we had rode on for a while, we halted under some trees, near a well and took dinner. Here our guide came to us four, who had missed our party, and said, that the man, whom he had sent after us, had lost his watch; and we four had to pay for it, each eight francs. I did not believe it immediately, but he kept on troubling us, until we finally paid it. This was another way of getting "bakchiche". The next day, another guide tried the same trick (to get "bakchiche") by saying, that he had lost his watch through having done some favor or other to some of our party. They would have kept on that way.

After dinner we left again, until, in the evening we came to Jenin, where our tents were pitched for that night on the Plain of Esdraelon, north-east of the village, which is surrounded by mountains; on the south are the Hills of Samaria; on the west, Mount Carmel; on the north-west, the Hills of Galilee, and on the north-east, the Mountains of Gilboa.

The next morning, Thursday April 25th, we made an early start and crossed the plain in two hours to Jezred, then down the valley for half an hour to Gideon's Fountain. After a one hour's ride from the fountain, a halt was made for lunch under the lemon trees at Shunem; then on to Endor and up to Nazareth. Here we passed the Mount of Precipice, thus called, because the Jews drove Christ out of a synagogue at Nazareth and led Him to this mount, from which they wanted to throw Him.

A little this side of Nazareth, the congregation met us, headed by Rev. Godfrey Schilling, O. S. F., the pastor, who immediately conducted us to the Church of the Annunciation. After having entered the Basilica, Father Godfrey ascended the steps that lead to the High Altar, welcomed and addressed us pilgrims, saying amongst other things: "You have now reached one of the principal sanctuaries of the Holy Land; when we are here in Nazareth, we fancy we see our Divine Saviour at every step we take!" After this we venerated the spot, where stood the Holy House, whereafter we put up at the Franciscan monastery.

Father Godfrey Schilling is a Franciscan and belongs to the province of St. John the Baptist, Cincinnati, Ohio. About eight years ago, before he left for Palestine, he came to see me. He returned to New York in the spring of 1891, and is now Assistant Commissary of the Holy Land for the United States, with Very Rev. Chas. Vissani at New York.

NAZARETH.

Nazareth is beautifully situated in a valley, surrounded on all sides by hills. It mostly contains stone houses, having flat roofs. From a distance it presents a good appearance. It numbers a population of about 5,000, and lies sixty-five miles north of Jerusalem. The Latin Church, called "Church of the Annunciation", is one of the finest in Palestine. Christ lived in Nazareth about thirty years, and for this reason it is so celebrated. It was in this humble village of Nazareth where St. Joseph and the Immaculate Virgin dwelt, and that the Son of God took upon Himself our human nature so as to accomplish our Redemption.

Church of the Annunciation.

The first morning of our stay in Nazareth, we said Mass in the Church of the Annunciation. When we came about to the centre of the church, we descended seventeen marble steps. Having reached the eighth step, we saw in the wall on each side of the staircase, a black stone, indicating the southern extremity of the Holy House. After descending six more steps, we were in a rectangular chapel, formerly occupied by the Holy House. Two altars are fixed against the northern wall; the one to the right dedicated to St. Joachim, and the one to the left, to the Archangel Gabriel. From this chapel we descended two steps by a pretty large passage between the altars and entered the Holy Grotto. This Grotto is entirely cut out in the rock, and, with the exception of the roof, lined with marble.

To the left, we saw the shaft of a pillar of red granite, which, it is said, indicates the place, where the Immaculate Virgin stood, whilst she spoke to the Heavenly Visitor. After the fire in the year 1630, some Africans, thinking that they might find a treasure concealed therein, broke it. It is now firmly fastened to the roof, being as it were, suspended from it. Between this pillar and the Altar of the Archangel Gabriel is another, indicating the place where the Angel stood, whilst delivering his divine message. Opposite thereto is an altar, dedicated to the Annunciation; above it is the Cross of the Holy Land, encrusted in a piece of white marble a few feet above the ground; beneath the altar, on the ground, we read on a tin star these words: "*Hic verbum caro factum est* (Here the Word was made Flesh)". I celebrated Mass on this altar. To the left of the Altar of the Annunciation, we ascended two steps into another chapel, not lighted from without, where an altar, dedicated to St. Joseph is fixed against the wall at its extremity, so that this altar and that of the Annunciation are back to back, both against the same wall.

From this last chapel we went by a staircase of thirteen steps to a grotto, which, according to a pious legend, was the kitchen of the Blessed Virgin.

We also went about 300 yards to the north-east of the Franciscan convent, to visit a chapel, newly built by the Franciscan Fathers on the ruins of a church, erected by the Crusaders on the site of the workshop of St. Joseph. About 100 steps north-west of the same convent is a chapel, built on the site of the synagogue, where Our Lord preached the Gospel and whence the inhabitants drove Him and attempted to throw Him from the top of the Mount of Precipice. From this synagogue, about 500 feet to the South-west, we visited a chapel, recently built by the Franciscans on the ruins of the more ancient chapel; here we saw a stone, covering almost the whole centre. This stone is called *Mensa Christi*; according to tradition, it served as a table for Our Lord and His disciples after the Resurrection.

THE VIRGIN FOUNTAIN.

About 400 steps from the Franciscan convent, at the north-eastern extremity of Nazareth, is the only fountain of this city; it is called the "Fountain of the Blessed Virgin", because she, according to tradition, came to this fountain for the water, necessary in her modest household. We all drank of it. The water comes by means of an aqueduct. We continually saw people, especially women, going to and fro, carrying jugs on their heads.

The Franciscan Fathers at Nazareth have a boys' school, and the Sisters an orphanage and girls' school, which are attended by a large number of Arabian children.

MOUNT THABOR.

Saturday morning, April 27th, we left for Tiberias, via Mount Thabor. We left Nazareth by the north-east side. After a few minutes we arrived on the heights, from which we could see Mount Thabor. But we were not there yet. In Palestine a person can see very far, because the atmosphere is so clear. After riding on for about two hours on a bad and stony road, we came to the foot of Mount Thabor. We began the ascent of the mountain by a path, which crosses a little ravine, then runs between green oaks and shrubbery, until we came to a well-cleared zigzag road. The ascent on horseback took one hour's time.

Mount Thabor is situated in the Plain of Esdraelon, six miles south-east of Nazareth in Galilee. It is noted as the scene of the Transfiguration of Christ. It is about 1900 feet high, limestone, and the sides are thickly covered with shrubbery of all kinds. A large portion of the plateau is covered with ruins and old walls. As we approach the summit and proceed, we pass between two walls; the one to the right belongs to the Franciscans where they have a small Convent and Chapel of the Transfiguration; the other to the left belongs to the Schismatic Greeks who also have a dwelling here.

Mount Thabor, separated from the other mountains, is higher than any of those which surround it. The Prophet Jeremiah compared Nabuchodonosor to it, saying: "As I live, (sayeth the King, Whose name is the Lord of hosts,) as

Thabor is among the mountains, and as Carmel by the sea, so shall he come" (Jeremiah, chap. xlvi, v. 18.)

This celebrated mountain is likewise mentioned in the Psalms. "Thabor and Hermon shall rejoice in Thy name." (Psalm lxxxviii, v. 13.)

It was on Mount Thabor, where Our Lord, before completing the work of our Redemption, gave some glimpses of His glory, in His Transfiguration, in presence of the three apostles, who were destined to witness His sufferings in the Garden of Gethsemane. On Mount Thabor His apostles were inspired and filled with enthusiasm, for they should encounter many hardships, before their pilgrimage was to be at an end. Our pilgrims on Mount Thabor were inspired and filled with enthusiasm in like manner, so much so, that they spoke of subscribing money to build a church on Mount Thabor, in honor of the "First American Catholic Pilgrimage to Palestine", and actually, a few hours later, a subscription list was drawn up, headed by Mr. Frank Headon with $500.00; others followed with $100.00 etc. In some way or another this matter was dropped again, as we, like the apostles, experienced harder times on our pilgrimage.

After remaining on the mountain for about one hour, during which time we took a little refreshment, we descended by the same road; some lead their horses, for fear of falling off. Coming down, we traveled on for about two hours until we came to a fountain, near which a tent was pitched, where we stopped to take dinner.

Father Godfrey, O. S. F., who had accompanied us here from Nazareth, took leave after dinner and returned to Nazareth.

At two o'clock P. M. we made a start for Tiberias.

THE LAKE OF GENESARETH OR TIBERIAS.

After having continued for about three hours north-east, we ascended a mountain, bringing us in sight of Tiberias, situated on the shores of a splendid lake of the same name. From here the road descends a very steep path. In about twenty-five minutes we reached the shores of the celebrated Lake of Genesareth, Sea of Galilee or Lake of Tiberias. On the side of the town of Tiberias our tents were pitched for the next two nights.

Tiberias has about 3,500 inhabitants, of whom about 400 are Catholics, the balance are Jews and Mussulmen. The Franciscan Fathers of the Holy Land have a hospital here. The church in which we said mass next morning, (it being Sunday), is dedicated to the Apostle St. Peter. According to tradition it stands on the spot where Christ said to St. Peter: "Feed my sheep". It was here also, that Christ gave to St. Peter the keys of heaven. Rt. Rev. Martin Marty, O. S. B., DD. of Sioux Falls, S. Dakota, is Bishop *i. p.* of this town. It is sixty-five miles north of the Dead Sea. Sunday morning about ten o'clock we went boat-riding on the beautiful Lake of Genesareth to Chorazin, Bethsaida and Capernaum. The lake is pear-shaped, being fifteen miles in length and six miles wide. From north to south the river Jordan flows through it, connecting it with the Dead Sea. Its water is clear and sweet and the hills that surround it are of a uniform brown color.

Our trip was most delightful, the lake being perfectly calm. Our guide informed us, that occasionally fierce, devastating storms arise suddenly, and apparently without provocation. History narrrtes, that such instances occurred already during the time of Christ, who was often on this lake. (Gospel St. Luke, chap. v, v. 1: "And it came to pass, that when the multitudes pressed upon Him to hear the Word of God, He stood by the Lake of Genesareth." V. 3: "And, going up into one of the ships, ... And behold, a great tempest arose in the sea, so that the boat was covered with waves but He was asleep." Matth., chap. viii, v. 24.) As we arrived at Capernaum, we left the boats to view the ruins, which are now virtually all that is left of that once famous city. On coming back, we passed a little hamlet called Magdala, because it is here where the Saint, according to tradition, was born. As we passed this place, we more than ever believed the words of the Gospel quoted above, as suddenly a great tempest arose on the lake, which frightened us considerably.

Monday morning April 29th, we returned to Nazareth. On leaving Tiberias we had a stony road, which, without being entirely bad, ascends to the north-west. Having been about an hour on the road, we reached the celebrated Plain of Hittine. This is the place where Our Lord multiplied the seven loaves and two fishes. Another half hour's journey brought us to the foot of the Mountain of Beatitudes. It was here where, according to the Jews, Jethro the father-in-law of Moses and great sacrificer of Madian was buried. It was on this Mountain that Our Lord preached the wonderful Gospel of the eight Beatitudes.

CANA OF GALILEE.

Having left the Mount of Beatitude about forty minutes, we were in sight of Cana. The first building we saw this side of it, was a ruined mosque, which marks the site of the dwelling of Nathanael. It was at Cana, of Galilee, that an officer, dwelling at Capernaum came to Jesus to beseech Him to restore his dying son to health. (St. John, chap. iv, v. 46: "He came again therefore into Cana, of Galilee, where he made the water wine. And there was a certain ruler whose son was sick at Capernaum.")

As we proceeded a little farther we were in the small town of Cana, where we took dinner at the monastery of the Franciscan Fathers. After dinner we went to the church, where Rt. Rev. Bishop Rademacher gave Benediction with the Blessed Sacrament. Cana is about four miles north-east of Nazareth. It is a small village of about 600 inhabitants. There are some Catholics here, but the most are Greeks and Mussulmen. It lies on the side of a hill, near to an excellent spring, which irrigates the surrounding country. Here we saw large cactuses, fig trees, olive and pomegranate trees, which prosper wonderfully. From Cana, going west, the road lies between two rows of cactuses. After having proceeded for an hour on a broken, stony road, almost southward, we reached a height in sight of Nazareth, and after descending the hill for about ten minutes, we passed before the Fountain of the Blessed Virgin, and in five minutes found ourselves again in Nazareth, where we sojourned for the night.

MOUNT CARMEL.

We left Nazareth Tuesday morning, April 30th, for Mount Carmel, and ascended a stony road towards the west; afterwards we turned north-west and lost sight of Nazareth. Proceeding on a bad road we at last came into the Plain of Esdraelon.

About an hour afterwards we stopped under one of our tents and ate dinner. From here, and ere this, we saw the heights of Carmel.

At two o'clock P. M., we went on, and crossed the River Kishon. About two hours after we had crossed this torrent, we came to Caifa, at the foot of Mount Carmel, toward the southern extremity of the beautiful Bay of St. John d' Acre. Several consuls have their residence here. Its population is 4,000, of which 1,000 are Schismatic Greeks; 600, United Greeks; 30, Maronites; 1,000, Jews; 170, Latins; the remainder Mussulmen. The interior of the city is dark and dirty, and surrounded by a wall. It took us about thirty minutes to ascend the heights of Carmel by a small stony road. We then continued on to the Carmelite Monastery on the western slope of Mount Carmel, where we put up for the night, and from where we had the finest view to be had in Palestine. Its highest elevation above the sea is 1,730 feet. Some years ago a German colony settled on the sides of Carmel, trying to cultivate the fertile soil. It was on Mount Carmel, that God confounded the ministers of Baal, through the Prophet Elias. This celebrated mountain was the residence of Elias, who kept his school there. The Holy Writ speaks of the beauty of Carmel. (Isaias, chap. xxxv, v. 2: "It shall bud forth and blossom and shall rejoice with joy and praise; the glory of Libanus is given to it, the beauty of Carmel and Saron; they shall see the glory of the Lord, and the beauty of Our God")

According to tradition, St. Anne herded flocks here, and had a residence for her shepherds, where she often came with the Blessed Virgin. Towards the year eighty-three, the hermits of Mount Carmel built a church there, which was dedicated to the Blessed Virgin. In 1245 Simon Stock, of Kent, England, after having lived for some time at Mount Carmel, became General of his Order and instituted at Rome the Confraternity of the Holy Scapular, in order to unite in one body, by exercise of piety, all who sought to honor especially the Blessed Virgin. In 1921, one hundred religious were massacred together on Mount Carmel, whilst singing the "Salve Regina." The infidels continued to torment and assail the Carmelites occasionally, until they massacred them in 1635. During the siege of St. John d' Acre, by Bonaparte, the Convent of Mount Carmel was converted into a hospital for the wounded, where this great General came to visit them. After the retreat of the French army, the Mussulmen came, and massacred all, leaving them unburied.

When the Carmelite Fathers returned to take possession, they found the bones of these victims, scattered over the mountain; they gathered them and had them buried in one grave, facing the gate of the convent, towards the sea, and placed over it a small pyramid. The Convent of the Carmelite Fathers is an immense square building, situated towards the extreme north-west of Cape Carmel. It contains a church, the exterior door of which faces the sea: Beneath the high altar, dedicated to the Blessed Virgin, is the Grotto of Elias (in this cave I said Mass), because it was formerly the dwelling of the great prophet. It is entered by a flight of five steps, and is fifteen feet long and nine feet wide. Above this cave is the high altar of this beautiful church, and above the high altar is a statue of the Blessed Virgin, representing her, reaching the Scapular of Mount Carmel to Simon Stock.

ST. JOHN D'ACRE.

The next morning, it being May 1st, we left Mount Carmel, leading our horses down another road, which was very steep. We visited another cave, which served as a school of the prophets, and then came through Caifa and rode along the beautiful Bay of St. John d' Acre. We arrived here at about twelve o'clock noon and ate dinner under our tent.

St. John d' Acre is a seaport of Syria, and is situated north of Mount Carmel, with about 5,000 inhabitants. It has a very good harbor.

In the afternoon we passed Sarepta, on our way to Sidon.

The next day we rode along the shores of the Mediterranean Sea up to Beyrout.

BEYROUT.

We arrived here Saturday, May 4th, at four o'clock P. M. This ended our long horse-back trip, and we were all glad of it, as we were very tired. We stopped at the Hotel d' Orient for three days. Beyrout is fifty-five miles north-west of Damascus, and there is a daily stage from here to Damascus. It has a population of about 100,000. The situation is beautiful, and the climate mild.

The streets in the suburbs are wide and passable for carriages. The houses are large and built of stone. It has a fine American college, and good bazaars. The American Protestants have their center here for their Missions in Syria. A great many Europeans are residing here. Its exports are grain, wool, cotton, raw silk, hides, tobacco, oils, hemp, drugs, figs and native wines. The last afternoon we were here, we went to the Convent of the Capuchin Fathers, and entered their church, where Rt. Rev. Bishop Rademacher addressed the pilgrims again, saying, amongst other things: "Since we have finished our blissful trip through the Holy Land, we should thank Almighty God once more for the graces bestowed upon us, and for having knelt at all the Holy Places with us." After this, Benediction with the Blessed Sacrament was given. Returning to our hotel, we ate supper, after which we took leave of the second section, who left for home the next day.

We left Beyrout Tuesday evening, at six o'clock, for Constantinople, on Austrian Lloyd Steamer "Diana." As we left the dock, we had to present our Turkish pass-port, which we bought in Jerusalem.

THE ISLAND OF CYPRUS.

The next day, after we left Beyrout, we passed the Island of Cyprus. It is a Turkish Island, and the most eastern of the Mediterranean. Towards the north it is about forty miles from the coast of Asia Minor. This island is about 150 miles long, and 50 miles wide.

The next day, Thursday, May 9th, at twelve o'clock noon, we passed the Island of Rhodes. It has a population of about 40,000, and is ruled by a Pasha, who holds office for life. We stopped here about two hours.

SMYRNA.

Friday, May 10th, at ten o'clock A. M., we arrived at Smyrna, where we stopped off to visit Ephesus. As soon as we reached the dock, we were asked for our pass-port; they were very strict with that. One man of our party could not find his, so some officers placed him in jail, although a friend of his went to the American Consul and explained the matter, whereupon, in the afternoon, he was set free again. After we finished presenting our Turkish pass-port, there were about fifty carriages in readiness, that took us to the depot, which was about a mile and a half distant, where after half an hour we took the train for Ephesus, in Asia Minor, which is fifty-four miles from here.

EPHESUS.

The country through which we passed here was level, and the soil fertile. There is a great deal of wine raised along where we passed through. A bottle of wine costs only eight cents, according to our American money. The railroad cars are like those of Europe and Egypt; they could be improved considerably.

After about two hours we came to Ephesus. At the station where we got off there are about five houses, amongst them a hotel and a restaurant. The ruins of the ancient, once renowned city are about a mile and a half from the station. As soon as we arrived we walked out to these.

On the way our guide now and then showed us some remnants of the city walls, Ephesus lies very low. I think we all suffered more from fatigue and heat, than even at the Jordan. Amongst the ruins we saw here, of any interest to us, was the Tomb of St. John the Evangelist, who was Bishop of Ephesus. Several of our party, including myself, knocked small pieces of marble off his tombstone. I was so much the more interested, since this beloved apostle of Our Divine Lord is also the Patron Saint of my church. We also saw some ruins of a large building, said to have been his church. On our way back to the station the ruins of the celebrated Temple of Diana were shown to us.

Diana, an ancient Italian divinity, in many respects corresponded with the Greek Artemis. Artemis was a twin sister of Apollo. She, like Apollo, sent plague upon men and animals. She was represented as a goddess. She was the goddess of the moon; also the guardian of young girls and women. She wore a long robe and veil, and loved to live in groves and at wells. Her statue was of ivory, and richly ornamented with gold.

The Temple of Diana, at Ephesus, was considered one of the seven wonders of the world. At the time St. Paul preached at Ephesus, in the year 54, it was the most notable thing in the city. St. Paul founded a Christian church here. It was also here, at Ephesus, that one of the most important Councils of the Church was held in the year 196, where the Bishops of Asia assembled, to fix the day for the celebration of Easter. Ephesus was furthermore adorned with a great theater, which held 50,000 persons. Ephesus is one of the twelve Ionian cities of Asia Minor.

In the year 356, the night on which Alexander the Great was born, the Temple of Diana was burnt by a certain Erostratus, who, by doing so, thought he would immortalize himself. The temple is said to have been 425 feet long, and 220 feet wide. It was four times as large as the Parthenon of Athens. After we had inspected the ruins of this magnificent and most wonderful temple, we repaired to the station and partook of some refreshments at the hotel, after which Very Rev. Chas. A. Vissany laid down on a bench in said hotel to rest a little; when it was time for us to go to the depot to make the train, he arose, and thinking and knowing there was no damage done by it, made motion to go, but the hotel-keeper thinking otherwise, told him, to his great surprise, that he had to pay three francs for resting on the bench, which, of course, *nolens volens* he had to pay. This was another way of getting "bakchiche."

About four o'clock P. M., the same day, we took the train back to Smyrna, arriving there about six o'clock. We again had carriages to take us to the dock. In driving along the sea, there was a strong breeze which blew Father Vissani's hat off; so he told one of the passers-by kindly to pick it up and reach it to him, but the fellow wanted to be paid before he would touch the hat, which then, of course, under the circumstances he got. On arriving here, we made for our steamer again, which was chartered for us.

SMYRNA.—CONTINUED.

The next morning some of us hired a guide and a carriage and drove through the City Smyrna, to see the most noteworthy things. We, as a matter of course, made a bargain with the guide for his service and the carriage before we started. When we returned three of us paid our share to Rev. George Meyer, the fourth member, and who had made the agreement, and he settled with the guide. So when he gave him the money agreed upon, the guide said that this was only for the carriage; he must be paid extra, he said, and furthermore, some of that money was counterfeit. He quarreled for quite a while, so I told Father Meyer to leave him go, and come along. We then went back to our steamer, this fellow following us all over it until it left. The distance from Beyrout to Smyrna is 700 miles. Smyrna is on the west coast of Asia Minor, 300 miles south-west of Constantinople. It has 200,000 inhabitants, of whom about 20,000 are Catholics. The greater part of the city stands upon a plain, and part of it on the slope of a hill, which gives it a very nice appearance. Its streets, in general, are narrow; it has a so-called caravan bridge with some ground around it, to accomodate camels at night. The Christians live mostly along the shore. The governor's palace, at Smyrna, is one of the principal buildings. It has also a beautiful Catholic Cathedral. The Catholics, Greeks and Armenians have each an archbishop residing at Smyrna.

There is a great deal of commerce carried on at Smyrna—important for steamers. Its harbor is magnificent and very much crowded. St. Polycarp was its first bishop. St. John in his Revelation speaks of seven churches; one of these was at Smyrna.

Our steamer left Smyrna for Constantinople Saturday, at eleven o'clock A. M. Our voyage on the Mediterranean Sea could not have been better.

THE DARDANELLES.

About six o'clock the next morning we passed the Dardanelles. They are castles built on the shores of the Hellespont, which joins the Agean Sea to the Sea of Marmora; it extends about forty miles. On its shore stood a city in ancient times called Dardanus, from which the name Dardanelles was taken. They are to guard the entrance to Constantinople, especially ships of war. Opposite, on the Turkish shore, to our left, as we went to Constantinople, we saw a great many soldiers and tents.

Before we entered the Dardanelles we passed a large man-of-war, which was there on guard. Xerxes united here the two continents with the bridge he built. At this place Alexander the Great crossed into Asia, and Leander swam across to visit Hero.

THE SEA OF MARMORA.

After we had passed the Dardanelles we came into the Sea of Marmora. This sea lies between European and Asiatic Turkey. It is about 160 miles long, forty-five miles wide and very deep. It is connected with the Black Sea by the Bosporus, and with the Archipelago by the Dardanelles. It contains several Islands, the principle one being the Island of Marmora, which is from ten to twelve miles long, one mile wide, and barren and hilly. It is known for its excellent marble and derives its name from the Latin term *marmor*.

CONSTANTINOPLE.

We arrived here at seven o'clock Sunday evening, the 12th of May. As the Turks allow no steamer to land or enter its harbor at night, so we remained on our steamer until the next morning, and we were glad it happened thus, because from the sea we had a much better view of Turkey's proud capital, than if we were within its walls.

The next morning we put foot on European soil. Here the custom officials did not interfere with our luggage, our guide having paid them a little, which made it all right. After we had landed in the Golden Horn, Constantinople's harbor, we were taken in carriages to Hotel Byzantine, a very roomy and elegant hotel. Constantinople is situated upon a triangular peninsula of the Europan shore. With all its suburbs it has about 1,000,000 inhabitants, the majority of which are Mussulmen. Constantinople, just at the junction of the Black and Mediterranean Seas is a great place for commerce; vessels of almost all nations lie in its harbors. The city is situated on hills, surrounded with villas; looked at from a distance, especially from the Sea of Marmora, it has, I may say, the finest harbor of any city I have seen; but when we find ourselves in the interior we are disappointed, like with all oriental cities. The streets, especially in the old city proper, are narrow, crooked and exceedingly dirty, and so irregular, that a stranger can hardly find his way through, in fact, it is almost impossible; as a general thing they have no names, are badly paved, and not lighted at night. Besides this there are thousands of ownerless dogs lying in the streets, which makes it very dismal especially at nighttime. With the sultan's residence are connected several more buildings, making it a small city of itself. Constantinople has about 500 mosques or prayer houses, and nearly 200 hospitals, in which provision is made also for Christians. For popular education there is not much done as yet. They have gas in some streets, and telegraphic connection especially with London. Communication with Scutari, situated on the Asiatic shore, is kept up with an immense number of kaiks (small boats). In its suburbs and in some streets of the city street railroads are operated.

THE TURKISH RAMADAN.

As soon as we came in sight of Constantinople there were several cannons discharged, it being about sunset. So we asked some of the officers on our steamer what that meant; they told us that the Turks celebrated their Ramadan (a month's fast). The regulations for fasting are very strict with the eastern Christians, especially with Armenians and Greeks. Mohammed appointed the ninth month at the Turkish year, as a four weeks' fast, which exists therein that no Mussulman is allowed to eat, drink or smoke from sunrise till sunset; the sick, weak and old are excepted; even these, although not bound by the regulation, observe it to some extent, for Mohammed considered fasting as the entrance to religion. The Koran was, according to them, revealed in this month, therefore it has been chosen by them as their month of fast. It is astonishing to see how strict the hard-laboring Turks observe the ordinance, so that in the greatest heat they will not even drink a dip of water. In the evening every Mussulman awaits with the greatest aspiration the setting of the sun. Sometimes, before the sun sets they hold eatables in their hands and watch till the sun disappears, and the cannon is discharged, which is a signal for them, that now the fast is over for that day; before that it is considered a forbidden fruit. But then they eat and drink until a late hour at night, and make up for lost time. When the sun rises the next morning their fasting begins again, and so on it continues for a month. This is called the Turkish Ramadan.

The Dogs.

A peculiar feature of Constantinople is its dogs, said to number 30,000. They are ownerless and rank next to the people in numbers. In all streets we meet a great number of large yellow dogs, which are lying and sleeping on the streets the greater part of the day. The Mussulman has great sympathy for the dog. The Koran prescribes to show great love even to the animals. They are partly looked upon by them as bringing them great luck, and partly because Mohammed led a great many dogs through the entrance of the sacred Romanus. It is an unquestioned fact that they keep the streets clean, by eating the excrement which is all thrown on the streets by the Orientals in that hot country. Although the Turks have, as said, a great veneration for the dogs especially, nevertheless none of them are allowed to be seen in the houses, consequently they are all ownerless. They are by no means good looking. They bear great similarity to the wolf and the fox, and are very poor and miserable looking. If you meet a dog on the streets you are not allowed to molest him, but must walk around him; even policemen leave them unmolested and walk around them. Very many are seen with one ear bit off, with only one eye, bruised neck, or hopping along on two or three legs. They form, as it were, a kind of a republic, and are divided into certain districts or precincts, having watches and guides, who diligently watch over the districts which they have once joined. Woe to the dog who tries to leave one district for another, without sufficient authority as it were; he is at once persecuted by the whole gang, and, if he is slow in departing, is killed by them. This persecution causes a very disagreeable noise at night. These dogs are also very often trampled upon by horses coming along the streets, or are run over by wagons since they do not move for anything.

Church of St. Sophia.

The most renowned mosque of Constantinople is without doubt the great Hagia Sofia, which was formerly a Catholic Church, in which several of her Councils were held. The Second General Council was held here A. D. 381, at which 150 bishops were present against the Arians. Then the Fifth General Council, to condemn the three chapters as they are known in the History of the Church, *v. g.*: (1) the person and writings of Theodore; (2) Theodoret's writings, in as far as the Nestorians were favored in them; (3) the letter of Ibas, which censured the Council of Ephesus.

Constantine was the founder of the Hagia Sofia. In 1453 it was changed into a mosque. It is built of brick, lined with the most beautiful colored marble; the ground plan is 350 feet long, and about 240 feet wide. The imposing dome is 110 feet in diameter, from below and up to the cupola 180 feet. The whole ceiling and its arches are inlaid and worked with splendid mosaic work and gilt. It has a gallery which is fifty feet wide, supported by sixty six columns, some of which, as is supposed, are from the temple of Diana, at Ephesus, the others of green jaspar. It is the grandest mosque we had seen so far.

The Bazaars.

Another peculiar feature of Constantinople, if not one of the most remarkable, and one well worth seeing, are its bazaars, which constitute a small city for themselves. The bazaars, or market halls, are large fire-proof buildings, lighted from above. The "Great Bazaar" is especially noteworthy. This immense building is a labyrinth of streets, lanes and alleys, in which hundreds of tradesmen sell their wares, and enclosing several covered streets. Each street has a special bazaar, each being occupied by a different trade. All concentrate in the principal bazaar, the walls and ceiling of which are decorated with variegated arabesques. The "Grand Bazaar" is a kind of resort for people during the hot summer days. It somewhat resembles a subterranean city, which on account of the dim light it receives from above, is veiled, as it were, in a constant semi-opaque. This is very conducible, as they can sell their goods even though they be somewhat damaged. In these half dark lanes or alleys we notice swarms of buyers, venders, guides, thieves and loiterers. Here we can see a wagon pass, there a horseman; here loaded camels enter, and between all this is the deafening noise of the salesmen, especially of the Greeks and Jews, who molest every stranger who passes by, by trying to sell him goods, one praising his goods more than another; one tries to pull you here, the other there, into his stoop, or store, reducing his price as you go on. From one side you receive an invitation from an Italian; from the opposite side you hear the Frenchman, the Greek, the Turk, the Arabian, the German or the English. It is a veritable Babel, in which your purse, if ever so well filled, almost suffers shipwreck, for the exposed thousandfold, most handsome and costly goods, are so inducive, that you are inclined and actually buy these articles for souvenirs.

In these bazaars a person can easily spend a whole day without getting tired or lonesome. Some of the veiled women inspect jewelry for hours before they find or know what they want, or we see them engaged in interesting conversation.

All the various goods, from Orient and Occident, are here exposed in hundreds of different shapes; you see the most splendid and costly goods and cloths in brokade, silk, linen, etc.; the most costly carpets from Smyrna and other cities and countries, the whole of which forms the most singular contrast imaginable. In some stores or shops we can see the finest display of Oriental slippers and Turkish pipes, called "Nargile." In short, the bazaars are a most wonderful market.

The Sultan's Drive to the Mosque.

Every Friday afternoon, the sultan drives to the mosque, not only for the performance of the prescribed prayers, but more especially to show himself to the people on this occasion; to let them know that he is still alive, for it is a well-known fact, that through the manifold conspiracies, many sultans have been killed in a most cruel manner; even the present sultan's predecessor was thus killed. From this duty no sultan can exempt himself. The present sultan, Abdul Hamed II., thus went to one of the mosques the Friday we were in Constantinople. Between twelve and one o'clock P. M., we went to the principal street where he was to pass, to observe the whole performance. Within an hour the street became so thronged with spectators, as to make it both unpleasant and fatiguing to the pedestrians. Every available portico and window was crowded to its utmost capacity by people, anxious to witness the passing of His Royal Highness. A regiment of 900 soldiers had been formed into platoons on each side of the thoroughfare, where the sultan was to pass. All along, the buildings were decorated with Mohammedan flags. On the day previous, the street had been covered with a layer of sand about four inches deep, over which the procession was to pass. At the head of the grand procession came several potentates from other cities and countries, last came the sultan in a carriage, drawn by four magnificent white Arabian steeds, at full speed.

Shortly before the sultan arrives at the mosque, a Muezzin ascends the gallery of the minaret, (a slender, lofty turret, on the mosque of Mohammedan countries, rising by different stages or stories and surrounded by one or more projecting balconies, from which the people are summoned to prayer) and sings with a loud voice which may be heard at some distance. The following are the words used in this song-prayer: "God is very great, I confess that Mohammed is the messenger of God! Come to prayer! God is great; there is no God, but God!" As the sultan is now in the act of ascending the stairs leading to the mosque the Turks all shout: "*Padisha tochok jasha*!" (That is: Long live the Padisha!) in the meantime, the sultan throws a glance at the people, saluting them in Turkish manner, by pointing his right hand to his forehead and heart. If an inferior of the turks salutes his supperior, he, besides pointing to his head and heart, also points at his feet, whilst saying: "*Salem aleikum*!" (Peace be with you!)

This imposing ceremony is indeed very ingenious, signifying: I am from head to feet thy friend and that with all my heart. After the sultan has performed his prayers, he returns to his carriage and proceeds home. The show being over, the crowd disperses.

THE MOHAMMEDANS.

Having entered so many mosques, or Mohammedan prayer houses and having seen them pray and perform their religious exercises, I think a few words on this subject may be in order. The religion is called Islem, meaning: full submission to God. Themselves, they call Moslems,—people of the Islem. Mohammed considered himself as a restorer of the religion God revealed to Abraham. He considered himself also as being sent by God, to induce his countrymen not to worship idols, but to worship his religion. The Jews were to adopt his new and final religion, which they were to embrace instead of the laws of Moses. The christians should not worship Christ as God. His teachings and laws were collected into his Koran (the sacred book of the Mohammedans, the chief authority in matters of faith, military or politics. It consists of fourteen chapters) The Mohammedans furthermore recognize the tradition which they trace to his companions, his wife and the first caliphs. The principal profession of faith of the Moslem is: There is but one God, and Mohammed is His prophet or apostle. They regard Christ only second to Mohammed. Those who blaspheme his name, are punished by death. They do not consider him as the Son of God, though his birth is considered as miraculous. They believe that he was taken to heaven, but another person suffered for him; they deny his crucifixion.

Their religion consists of the following four rules: (1) Purification and prayer; (2) almsgiving; (3) fasting; (4) the pilgrimage to Mecca. Before prayer they wash. The Moslems pray soon after sunset, at nightfall, at day break, and in the afternoon. Five times a day they are called to prayer by the Muezzins, from the minarets of the mosques. While praying they must hold their face towards Mecca. Every mosque has a niche in the wall nearest to Mecca. All Moslems should make a pilgrimage to Mecca at least once during life.

THE DERVISHES.

In Constantinople we also saw a great many derwishes, in fact it was the only place where we saw them. Dervish, or Dervise signifies poor; they are only seen in Mohammedan cities or countries, and are a kind of monks. There are several classes or orders of dervishes. They usually live in monasteries, although some of them live with their families in villages. They are forbidden to beg, their law obliging them to support themselves by labor. All are allowed to marry and live outside the convents, but must live in the monastery two nights each week. According to their religious rules they must mortify their flesh, pray and dance. They hold their religious meetings Tuesdays and Fridays, and observe the Ramadan very strictly. They wear coarse robes and go bare-legged.

The Order of the Mevlevis, who are the most numerous, are not allowed to marry, and must live in the monasteries. They are also known as "Whirling Dervishes." They have fantastic dances, in which they whirl around very rapidly to the sound of a flute; when the music ceases they stop at once or dance until they drop from exhaustion. Mevlevi was their founder, in memory of whom they dance. While, as they say, his companion Hamza, played the flute, he, being without food, turned around miraculously for four days.

Then there are the "Howling Dervishes," who sway their bodies backward and forward until their mouths foam and they fall to the ground, in the meantime pronouncing the name of Allah (God).

THE BOSPORUS.

The Bosporus is the channel which joins the Black Sea and the Sea of Marmora, between Europe and Asiatic Turkey. It is so narrow that an ox can swim across. It is about fifteen miles long and two miles wide, and where it is the narrowest it is about half a mile wide. We took a boat ride on this strait one afternoon, up to the Black Sea. Along the sides of the channel there are beautiful castles and ancient ruins as well as splendid buildings of the present day. According to tradition the channel or strait was formed by the bursting of the barriers of the Black Sea.

ATHENS, GREECE.

After having spent about eight days in Constantinople, we left Monday, May the 20th, at half past five o'clock in the evening, and took a steamer for Athens. The next morning about six o'clock a cannon was discharged on our steamer as a salute to some soldiers, who were in a small city on an island.

Wednesday morning, May 22d, at five o'clock, we arrived at Pireus, the seaport of Athens, which has a population of about 15,000. Here we took carriages for Athens, which is five miles distant from Pireus. The distance from Constantinople to Athens is about 380 miles.

Athens is at present the capital of the Kingdom of Greece. It has 110,000 inhabitants. The present City of Athens is very pretty, some of its principal streets being over 100 feet wide. The principal houses, and in fact, nearly all houses, are built of white, intermixed with a kind of sand color stone. The principal houses are only about fifty years old. There is quite a contrast between the Oriental cities and streets, and those of Athens. In the Royal

Palace of King George, there are three different chaplains: the kind has a Lutheran, the queen a Russian, and the children a Greek chaplain. The present archbishop of Athens is the first bishop Athens has had for 300 years. When His Grace was asked by us, what he thought of the Jews and Schismatic Greeks, and about their conversion, he answered that he is of the opinion that the Jews would be converted fifteen minutes before the last judgment, and the Greeks five minutes after the last judgment.

The Theatre of Dionysus.

We then went to see the Theatre of Dionysus, which we reached at the level of the broad passage encircling it. Above, to the right, rise the columns, which once bore triumphal tripods; below is a grotto, now dedicated to "Our Lady of the Golden Grotto," whence the remains of the choragic monument of Thrasyllus, destroyed by a bombardment in 1827, are invisible. The rows of seats are only preserved in the lower part of the theater, which was excavated in 1862. The most interesting is the lowest tier, which was the priest's, constructed of marble, and with the seat for the priest of Dionysus in the middle. After having been long contented to employ wooden scaffoldings, the Athenians founded a stone theatre in the year 500 B. C., but it remained unfinished till the time of Lycurgus. The stage, with the semi-circular orchestra in front of it, was the portion chiefly altered, so that little probably now remains of that, on which Eschylus and Sophocles exhibited their dramas. The theatre is divided into thirteen sections, one for each of the thirteen "Phylae" or tribes, and was capable of holding upwards of 30,000 spectators. The wall of the stage is adorned with good reliefs and stooping Sileni as supporters. The theatre lies in the sacred district of Dionysus, to whose temple the foundations at the back of the stage probably belonged. Here, too, stands the circular altar of Dionysus, which was formerly in the orchestra. To the west of the theatre are two terraces, extending along the south side of the Acropolis, both of which were excavated a few years ago. On the upper one stood the Asklepieum or sanctuary of Esculapius, afterwards converted into a Christian church, and now almost entirely destroyed. The reliefs and sculptures found here are preserved in the hut to the left, in the exterior court of the Acropolis. On the lower terrace was situated the Stoa, which extended to the "Odeum of Herodes Atticus." About half way up to the left of the path, is situated the Arcopagus, a rugged mass of rock which still retains its ancient name. The sixteen steps found here, are those which the judges of the Arcopagus, the highest judicial tribunal at Athens ascended to their nocturnal sessions. The two spaces on the summit afforded the sole and somewhat limited accomodation for judges, prosecutors and defendants. From here a fair view is had over the city and the plain. In the profound and gloomy ravines, at the base of the abrupt precipice, on the north, was situated the shrine of the Erinnyses. This was probably the spot on which St. Paul stood when preaching to the Athenians.

The Acropolis.

Passing round the wall which supports the Temple of Nike, we stood before the Propylaea, the grand entrance to the Acropolis, with its numerous temples called "a votive offering to the gods." The ancient city was built round a central rocky height, called Acropolis, which was elevated about 320 feet above the level of the city, and 600 feet above the Mediterranean Sea. We all ascended the Acropolis. The Pelagians, the traditional aboriginal inhabitants of Attica, are said to have leveled the upper part of the rock and rendered its sides more precipitous by artificial means, while they protected the only accessible entrance on the west side by an outwork with nine gates. The castle then became the residence of the kings of Athens; justice was administered at the gates of their palace, and the principal temples were in the vicinity. The courts of judicature and public offices were afterwards transferred to the lower part of the city, while the castle remained sacred to the gods. There was erected at the side of the Parthenon a temple of Athens, called Hekatompedos or "the hundred-footed," so named on account of its vast dimensions. There was also a more magnificent entrance to the Acropolis erected, both of which were however destroyed by the Persians in 4807. Pericles, however, conceived the idea of restoring the temples of the gods, to whom Greece apparently owed her preservation, and to erect imperishable memorials of the glory of Athens. Accordingly, in 448, vast building operations were commenced on the Acropolis. Within the short space of ten years the Parthenon was completed and the Propylaea were erected. These structures were a marvel of architectural talent, and stood almost uninjured till the eighteenth century.

The highest point of the plateau (500 feet above the level of the sea; 360 yards long and 180 yards wide) was occupied by the Parthenon, *i. e.*, the Temple of the Virgin Athene, and it continued to be sacred to that goddess until the sixth century of our era. It was then converted into a church dedicated to the virgin, and in 1205 was made the Roman Catholic Metropolitan Church of Athens by the Franks.

In 1459 the Parthenon became a Turkish mosque; after the unfortunate explosion, caused by the Venetians in 1687, a smaller mosque was erected among the ruins. The Parthenon was discovered in this condition by an English Ambassador, in 1801, who caused a considerable portion of the frieze, and the best statues to be carried off. The fragments that now remain are still the greatest ornament of the Acropolis.

The Propylaea, which was erected within five years, consisted of a vast arched entrance-gateway, with two unequal wings, a masterpiece of inventive talent and perfect workmanship, and regarded by the ancients as the gem of the Acropolis, superior even to the Parthenon itself.

The Erechtheum, the third important ruin of the Acropolis, comprised within its ample precincts the most ancient and venerable shrines of Athens. Here Pallas Athene, the goddess of Athens, and her first priestess Pandrosus, were revered; here, too, were the sacred olive trees planted by Athene. The structure was partially restored after its destruction by the Persians. The delicacy of the Ionic columns and the ornamentation is admirably in keeping with the moderate proportions of the edifice. It was converted into a church at the same period as the Parthenon. From the 13th to the 15th century it was the residence of the Franconian dukes, and after that it was occupied by the harem of the Pasha.

THE OLYMPIEUM.

South-east of the Acropolis was the Olympieum, the largest, and as it seems, the most magnificent temple of Athens. Its construction with some intervals required a period of 700 years. It was 355 feet long, 175 feet wide, and very high, being surrounded by 160 columns, sixteen of which can be seen to this day; they are five feet in diameter and more than sixty feet high.

THE THESEUS.

This temple is the best preserved monument, which gives us, I may say, the best idea of the splendor of ancient Athens. It was built of Pentelic marble, being 105 feet long and forty-six feet wide. The sides were adorned with exquisite sculptures, some of which can still be seen, although they are considerably injured; many were painted, as were also portions of the building representing incidents from the life of Theseus, son of Egeus, King of Athens. This Egeus is said to have united the twelve cities, into which Attica was formerly divided, into one political body.

THE PROPYLAEA.

This structure consisted of three portions: the central gateway, and the two colonnades, situated towards the west and east in front of the wall containing the gates themselves. Above each of these and on both sides arose pediments, and each was borne by six Doric columns, thirty-one feet high and four feet thick, the intercolumniation, where the road passed through, being fourteen feet in width, whilst the other columns were about seven feet apart. The depth of the west portico, rising boldly on a basement of four steps, on the slope of the hill, was forty-five feet, and it was supported by two rows of slender Ionic columns, three in each, thirty-six feet high and three feet thick. Fragments of the capitals still lie in the colonnade; the wall with the five steps higher, the highest of which consists of bluish Eleusinian marble. The quadrangular apertures were formerly surrounded with rich decorations. The six columns of the east colonnade were another step higher, and twenty-three feet distant from the wall with the gates. The huge stone beams which spanned this wide space, as well as those which extended from the north and south walls of the west portico to the Ionic columns, are among the largest hewn stones in existence, and were universally admired by the ancients. Even this approach to the Acropolis was profusely adorned with statues and reliefs, to which the three draped Graces, executed by Socrates, and the Hermes Propylaeus belong. Architectural relics, inscriptions, and fragments of statues now lie here in confusion. The two wings of the Propylaea project twenty-six feet towards the west. In front of the north wing is a portico thirteen feet in depth, surrounded by the columns between the "antae" *i. e.*, the columns immured in the bounding walls. Beyond this is a quadrangular space thirty-seven feet in depth, lighted by windows above, and called the Pinacotheca, from having been used as a gallery for pictures by celebrated masters. The edifice, as far as the frieze, as well as its substructure, is admirably preserved; but the roof was destroyed in the Middle Ages when one story was added. Among the numerous relics preserved here, the most interesting are the small reliefs which once adorned inscriptions recording the rendering of the accounts of public officials, and which show us the form of the celebrated Statue of Athene in the Parthenon, executed in gold and ivory, by Phidias. To the west the antae is still preserved, and on the marble slabs are traces of a buttress, a corner column, and an iron railing between them. The wall of polygonal blocks here, is a relic of the ancient Pelagic fortress. Passing through the Propylaea, we ascend the great slope of the Acropolis, now a vast field of ruins, presenting a profoundly impressive scene. Here we had an imposing view of the Parthenon, rising above all, the charming Erechtheum with its rich sculpture and brilliant coloring, and the numerous smaller shrines; then the profusion of votive offerings and the forest of statues and groups which greeted the eye here when the bronze gates of the Propylaea were opened to admit the Panathenaean procession, in which nearly all the inhabitants of Athens took part to carry to the Temple of Athene, a crocus-colored garment of the goddess, in which were woven representations of her victorious deeds. This procession is represented in the frieze of the Parthenon. The numerous square depressions, of various sizes, in the rock, all mark the spots where votive offerings were placed, while the pedestals, scattered about on every side, were once adorned with statues. Thus, adjoining the south column of the east colonnade, is the basement of a statue of Athene (Athene as the goddess of health), to commemorate the marvelous fact that the goddess had appeared to the sculptor Pyrrhus in a dream, and prescribed a remedy for a favorite slave who had been injured during the building of the Propylaea.

The Parthenon.

The Parthenon was intended to form the crowning feature of the Acropolis, and to have this effect also when viewed from below. It is therefore situated at the north-east angle, on the culminating point of the rocky plateau. On the summit of the rock, on the south side, was a vast substructure of porous stone, twenty-one feet in height, on which the marble "*stylobates*" (a pillar or column), six feet in height arose in three steps. The bases of the columns of the Parthenon were therefore nearly on a level with the summit of the Propylaea. The steps are not perfectly horizontal, but slightly convex. The upper surface 243 feet long and 108 wide, supported by eight columns at each extremity, and seventeen at each side (the corner columns being counted twice), in all, forty-six columns, thirty-six feet high and six feet in diameter. In the east portion, 104 feet long, and sixty-seven feet in width, in the Parthenon proper, stood the gold and ivory statue of Athene, forty-seven feet in height, the most admired work of Phidias. The nude portions were of ivory, the rest of the statue, and the removable mantle of gold.

The goddess was represented standing, holding a spear in her right hand, and on her extended left a victory six feet in height; by her left side rested her shield, on which a snake was entwined and on her head was a helmet adorned with sphinxes. At the sides were two rows of Doric columns, three feet thick, there being nine in each row. In the west part, which was connected with the east portion by two small doors and supported by four Ionic columns, the treasury of the state was deposited. On the north and south side of the Parthenon, the ruins lie in picturesque confusion.

The Erechtheum.

To the north of the Parthenon is situated the "Erechtheum", the external form of which is still distinctly traceable, but the internal arrangements have been completely concealed by subsequent alterations. Three vestibules led to the interior, which was sixty-six feet long and thirty-five feet wide. The variety, exhibited in its architecture, was a great charm of this temple.

The east colonnade, an ordinary pronaos of six Ionic columns, twenty-seven feet high and two feet in diameter, formed the entrance to the temple of Athene; it contained a sitting figure of the goddess, with the eternal lamp.

The north vestibule had four Ionic columns in front, laid eight feet deeper than the east colonnade, while its columns measured six inches more in diameter and were three feet higher. The two peculiar apertures below the vestibule, are said to have been caused by the trident of Poseidon, when he caused the salt-spring to flow by striking the rock. The door, which is still well-preserved, here led to a passage to the other temples, which were lighted by three windows, introduced between the Ionic half-columns in the west wall. The small door farther west in the same colonnade, led to the sacred precincts of the goddess, which extended towards the north-west as far as the entrance to the so-called "*Agraulus Grotto*" on the north wall of the Acropolis. The Persians are said to have gained access by this entrance to the ill-defended stronghold. At a subsequent period the priestess of Athene decended by this door to the shrine of Agraulus which was below. The south portico is called the "Hall of the Caryatides." The figures supporting the beams were simply termed "maidens" by the Athenians.

The statues, somewhat exceeding life-size stand on pedestals, eight feet in height, and bear on their heads ornaments resembling capitals.

The external wall of the temple was adorned with frieze, representing figures of white marble on a ground of Eleusinian stone, above which ran a beautiful cornice of palm leaves.

THE COSTUMES OF GREECE.

Costumes in great variety render walking in the streets of Athens very entertaining to the stranger.

The national Greek, or rather, Albanian costume, consists of a high fez, with long, blue tassel; a blue or red jacket, with open sleeves and richly embroidered; a vest of similar description; shirt, with wide and flowing sleeves; a leather belt, with a pouch for weapons; the white *fustanella*, short breeches; red gaiters, and pointed red shoes.

The inhabitants of the islands wear a different costume, which is of a Turkish origin; high fez, worn upright; short dark-colored jacket; red vest, and short, wide trousers of dark green or blue calico; legs sometimes bare, and shoes with buckles.

The Cretan costume is similar, but high boots are worn instead of shoes. In cold or wet weather a cloak, with a hood made of goats' hair, is worn by all classes.

The women generally wear French clothing, but sometimes adorn their heads with a fez, with a gold tassel. The Albanian peasant women alone still retain their national costume, consisting of a long petticoat, embroidered on the sleeves and skirt, with a short, white woolen dress above it; they adorn their hair and necks with chains of coins, strung together.

During our stay at Athens we also visited the ruins of the Temple of Jupiter, of which a few massive columns, about sixty feet high and four feet in diameter, are still standing, while others, yet well preserved, are lying on the ground. We saw also the Theatre of Bacchus.

THE GULF OF CORINTH, OR LEPANTO.

We left Athens May the 23d by rail for Corinth and Patras. About midways from Athens to Patras is Corinth. There is nothing left of this once renowned city.

There is a canal being made between the Gulf of Athens and the Gulf of Corinth, so that from the Gulf of Athens the steamers can go through the canal, on through the Gulf of Corinth, or Lepanto, and on to Brindisi, Italy. We saw them work at the canal. At present steamers must go around from Pireus to Patras, which requires several days.

After we had passed Corinth, we had the Gulf of Corinth, or Lepanto, to our right, where the battle of Lepanto took place, and, strange to say, as we passed along the gulf (afternoon of May 23d, between three and five o'clock) we recited our Vespers of the Feast of *Auxilium Christianorum*, as the battle was fought on this gulf.

Lepanto, is a seaport of Greece, on the north coast of the gulf of the same name, twelve miles north by east of Patras, and it has a population of about

4,000. In the Middle Ages Lepanto was for a long while in possession of the Venetians, who fortified it and sustained a siege by the Turks in 1477, lasting four months, and during which the besiegers lost 30,000 men.

The Gulf of Lepanto, also called Gulf of Corinth, is between the north coast of the Morea and the mainland of Greece, and is about seventy-five miles long from east to west. The Gulf of Patras at its west end is connected with it by a strait more than one mile in width, called the Strait of Lepanto, or Little Dardanelles. In the middle the Gulf of Lepanto is about sixteen miles wide, and it is surrounded by picturesque mountains. There was a most important battle fought here. In 1571 there was a war between the Turkish Sultan Selim II. and Philip II., King of Spain, Pope Pius V. and the Republic of Venice. The three Christian powers fitted out a great army under the command of Don John, of Austria. The armies met at Messina, in Sicily, consisting of 300 vessels of large size, 50,000 seamen, 20,000 Spanish and 9,000 Italian soldiers. They sailed from Messina September 16th and reached the entrance of the gulf October 7, 1571, where they came in sight of the Turkish fleet, who had 250 royal galleys of very large size, and a great many small vessels, containing in all 120,000 men. The Christian fleet was three miles long. The right wing was commanded by Doria, a Genoese admiral; the left wing was commanded by a Venetian admiral, and the centre by Don John personally, who was assisted on the one side by the Papal captain-general, and on the other by a Venetian general. Previous to the battle, Don John rapidly passed through the fleet, saying to his men: "You have come to fight the battle of the Cross—to conquer or to die. But whether you are to die or conquer, do your duty this day, and you will secure a glorious immortality." The battle resulted in the total defeat of the Turks, of whose fleet 130 galleys were taken and eighty burnt and sunk. They lost about 30,000 men, of whom 5,000 were taken prisoners. This victory astonished whole Christendom, as it was one, won over the Turks, who, before this battle, were considered invincible at sea. When the Pope heard of this victory he burst into tears, and said: "There was a man sent by God, whose name was John." The Turks, upon this defeat, were entirely disheartened.

We arrived at Patras about seven o'clock the same evening and ate supper, after which we took the steamer across the Adriatic Sea to Brindisi, Italy, passing the Island of Corfu during the night.

BRINDISI.

We arrived at Brindisi Saturday morning at two o'clock. As soon as we had landed we had to go through the custom house. This being Italy again they were more strict than in any other country; even on things we had bought in Italy on our way to Palestine, we now, on our return, had to pay duty again. When we told them that we had bought these things in Italy they said to us: "We don't believe it." These officials wanted Rt. Rev. Bishop Rademacher to pay three francs and a half for his cassock.

Brindisi is a seaport of Italy, situated at the head of a deep and sheltered harbor of the Adriatic Sea. It has a population of about 16,000. There is here comparatively little of interest to the traveler. It has a strong and well-located fortress, with strong towers. Its cathedral, a Norman structure, has been much injured by earthquakes.

The prosperity of Brindisi has greatly increased since the completion of the railway along the eastern coast from Northern Italy. It now has connection with all railways of the continent; the mail steamers to the East also embark from here.

In the afternoon at five o'clock we took the train for Loreto.

LORETO.

The next morning, Sunday, May 26th, at five o'clock, we arrived at Loreto. It was not in our program to stop at Loreto, but a few days previous we told our guide we would like to stop off a day at Loreto, and so he made arrangements and left us off. Here Monsignor Staniero, from Rome, came to meet us again. Having arrived at the station of the same name, we took carriages and drove up about a mile and a half to the little town of Loreto, situated on a hill.

Loreto is three miles from the Adriatic and twelve miles south of Ancona. Its population numbers about 15,000. It is renowned as the site of the celebrated sanctuary of the Blessed Virgin Mary, called *Casa Santa*, or Holy House, in which the annunciation and incarnation took place, and in which the Holy Family dwelt at Nazareth upon their return from Egypt. May 10,

1291, this Holy House was miraculously transported by angels from Nazareth to Teraste, Dalmatia, on the east coast of the Adriatic, whence, the 10th of December, 1294, it was carried to the coast of Italy to Recanati, and finally to Loreto on the lands of a lady named Lauretta, from whom the town took its name, and where it is now held in great veneration. The *Casa Santa* is a rudely built stone house, the walls inside being put up like a well is walled up, not plastered, cemented or white-washed. The house is about thirteen feet high, twenty-seven feet long and twelve feet wide, with one door. In a niche over the fire-place is a statue of the Blessed Virgin, attributed to St. Luke. On February 10, 1797, the French carried this statue to Paris, but Napoleon returned it to Pius VII. This pope enriched it with precious stones and sent it back to Loreto on December 9, 1802. The Holy House contains a great many relics and treasures. The outside of it is covered with exquisite sculptures in relief. Beneath the high altar is a stone, on which the apostles are said to have celebrated Mass. There is a beautiful altar inside the Holy House, on which the most of our priests, including myself, said Mass; then there is an altar outside, but against the wall of the Holy House, on which the remainder of the priests said Mass, who did not wish to wait until they could all say Mass inside the House, as it would have made it very late for the last ones. A vessel was also shown to us in the Holy House, out of which, according to tradition, the Holy Family should have eaten. The Bishop of Loreto held it in his hand, placed our religious articles therein and blessed them. On the top of the Holy House there is also a small bell, with which, for the first time, the Angelus was rung. Rt. Rev. Bishop Rademacher asked the Bishop of Loreto to be kind enough and have it rung for us pilgrims, and he did so. The Litany of the Blessed Virgin, called the Lauretan Litany, originated here.

We left Loreto Sunday evening at five o'clock and took the train for Venice.

VENICE.

We arrived at Venice Monday morning at five o'clock. From Brindisi to Venice we traveled two nights in succession, without sleeping five minutes. As soon as we landed we were taken to our hotel in gondolas (a flat-bottomed pleasure boat, very long and narrow, used on the canals in Venice).

Venice is the capital of the province, and is situated on the Gulf of Venice; thus the north-western part of the Adriatic is called, which is 156 miles east of Milan and 250 miles north by west of Rome. It has a population of about 140,000. It is located in the midst of lagoons (a marsh, shallow pond or lake, especially one into which the sea flows), originally formed by the retreating of the sea. In Venice there are over one hundred canals. Communication is further kept up by small streets, lanes, alleys and courts, which are nearly all poorly paved, and by 400 bridges. There is a viaduct at Venice about two miles long, which has more than 200 arches, and which connects Venice with the principal railways at the junction of Mestre.

The city is divided into two unequal parts by the *Canalazzo*, or Grand Canal, which is spanned by two iron bridges. Along the Grand Canal are more than 4,000 magnificent buildings, erected along the water's edge, and painted black. The city from all sides seems to float on water.

St. Mark's Square.

St. Mark's Square is the most beautiful and animated part of Venice; it is about 580 feet long and 270 feet in greatest width. Along here are the cathedral, the doge's palace, and other magnificent buildings. St. Mark's Church is the most important of all churches in Venice. It is of Byzantine style, some of its marble pillars having been brought from the East. Above the principal portal are the celebrated bronze horses, brought from Constantinople in 1205; Napoleon carried them away to Paris in 1797, but in 1815 restored them to Venice.

The Cathedral of Venice has five domes, the main one being ninety feet, the others eighty feet high. The interior is exceedingly rich, having precious marble columns and rich mosaics upon a gold ground.

During our stay at Venice we also inspected the famous Bridge of Sighs, which connects the palace with the *carceri, i. e.* public prison. The palace of the great judicial dignitaries of the republic fills nearly the whole north side of St. Mark's Square; it stands upon fifty arches and is one of the greatest structures of Venice.

The custom house is also a notable building, but most impressive of all, I may say, is the arsenal and dock-yard, situated in the east end of the city. Here are docks, a long rope-walk, founderies and other works; the whole is surrounded by a splendid wall, which is more than three miles in circumference, and at the erection of which more than 16,000 men were employed.

At the land entrance are lions of marble, which were brought from Greece at the end of the 17th century.

The celebrated vessel, which was annually used in the doge's so-called marriage with the Adriatic, by throwing a ring into the sea, was destroyed by the French in the 18th century.

In Venice, near the cathedral, is also a remarkable and high tower, over the dial of which are two bronze figures, known as "Moors", which strike the hours on a bell.

According to tradition, the bones of St. Mark, the Apostle, were transferred A. D. 829 from Alexandria to Venice. He was made the Patron Saint of the republic, which is often called "Republic of St. Mark."

We left Venice for Milan, Tuesday May the 28th, at nine o'clock A. M. We were taken to the railroad station in gondolas.

At Mestre Junction, which is connected with Venice by a viaduct, two miles long and having more than 200 arches, we took the train for Milan.

MILAN.

Between Venice and Milan the country is level and beautiful.

We arrived at Milan, which is 160 miles west of Venice, at four o'clock in the afternoon, and were then taken to our hotel in street cars. After a short while, I and one more of our pilgrims had to go to the custom house; out of all the trunks, the officials had selected ours for examination, and the other trunks were immediately taken to the hotel.

Milan is the capital of the province and has a population of far over 200,000. It lies south of the Alps and is situated in a fertile plain. It is one of the most pleasant cities of Europe. The city is almost circular. There is a street, called *Strada di circonvallazione*, which encircles the city and is more than ten miles in length; in a thoroughfare we rode the whole length of above named street. Some of the streets are narrow, but generally well-paved. The *Piazza Borromeo* is a fine street, and is adorned with a statue of St. Charles Borromeo. The street called *Corsi*, which leads to the principal gates, is the most fashionable. The houses are generally from three to five stories high.

Among the most remarkable buildings of Milan are the palace of the government, the palace of art, the palace of justice, the *palazzo della Corte*, the residence of the king when he visits Milan, and the archiepiscopal palace; but all of these are greatly surpassed by the *duomo* or cathedral.

The Cathedral.

This cathedral is, next to St. Peter's at Rome, the largest church in Italy. It is located on the *Piazza del Duomo*, and almost in the centre of the city. It is not yet completed, although the main design is carried out. The interior is crowded with different monuments of Saints and princes. As far as it pertains to carving and statuary, this cathedral eclipses all churches in the world; its ornamentation is so profuse, that much of the effect is lost.

The cathedral is more than 500 feet in length; breadth of body, 260 feet, between the walls of the transept, 290 feet; width of nave, from centre to centre of the columns, seventy feet, which is double the width of the side aisles; height of nave, 165 feet. The interior is divided into a nave and four aisles by four ranges of clustered pillars. It has 100 large pillars, which are forty-five feet in circumference and sixteen feet in diameter: each is formed of eight shafts, eighty feet high, *viz.*: a base, four feet; shaft, fifty-eight feet, and the capital, eighteen feet. The diameter of each of the shafts, which support the arches of the roof, is eight feet. The windows of the cathedral are 100 feet high. The pavement is laid in mosaic, in red, blue and white marble.

The entire structure is built of white marble, the exterior having niches and pinnacles for 4,500 statues, of which more than 3,400 are now completed. The cathedral has twelve altars; above the high altar is one of the true nails with which Christ was nailed to the cross; it is fastened to the ceiling for fear of it being stolen. I and several of our pilgrims went up into one of its highest steeples; the height of it was more than 400 feet.

Beneath the floor, in the basement is a chapel and an altar over the remains of St. Charles Borromeo, who was Bishop of Milan; his body was shown to us. I said Mass on this altar. As the Ambrosian Rite is in force here, we, of the Latin Rite could say Mass only on this altar. The chalice and the monstrance, which St. Charles Borromeo used, were shown to us, as was also his ring, his mitre, which Pope Leo XIII. presented to this cathedral on his golden jubilee, and a vestment and stole, which was presented by Pope Pius IX.

Another of the most remarkable churches of Milan is that of St. Ambrose, which we also visited. This church is renowned for its antiquity. In it Ecclesiastical Councils were held and the sovereigns crowned. Here we saw the tomb of St. Ambrose and his marble chair. I sat in this chair. In the rear of the altar is the choir, and the pulpit (or at least where it stood), from whence St. Augustine was converted. I ascended this pulpit. The "*Te Deum*" was composed here.

We left Milan May the 30th at seven o'clock in the morning, *via* Como and the St. Gothard Tunnel for Lucerne, Switzerland.

After we had left Milan about one hour, we came to Como, a province of Italy. The province is bounded on the north by Switzerland, and on the south by Milan. Como is the capital of the province. The city is situated at the south end of the Lake of Como twenty-five miles north-west of Milan.

Having left Como, we shortly came to St. Gothard's Tunnel; it took us about twenty minutes to pass through.

ST. GOTHARD'S TUNNEL, SWITZERLAND.

The boring of this tunnel was begun at Airolo and at Goeschenen at the same time, in the year 1870. It is the longest railroad tunnel in the world. The St. Gothard's Tunnel is a little more than nine miles in length. In 1882 it was finished and formally opened, the first passenger train passing through it in fifty minutes. It is about twenty-four feet wide and twenty feet high and in the main tunnel two tracks are laid. The leading idea in constructing it, was to connect the North Sea with the Mediteranean Sea, by the most direct route and consequently it had to be built through the chain of the Alps. It was to preserve for Switzerland its share of the traffic between North European and

Italian ports. Engineers pronounce the St. Gothard Tunnel the greatest work executed by man. It was built by Switzerland, Italy and Germany. The cost was estimated at 180,000,000 francs. France looked upon its completion with feelings of envy, as it was feared that considerable freight would be lost to it from the North Sea to the Mediterranean Sea. The tunnel was built by a Swiss company.

Within a distance of about 125 miles from the Lake of Zug to the frontier of Italy, we passed through fifty other tunnels. The railroad track for nearly half the way is subterranean between Brunnen and Fluellen, where it skirts the Lake of the Four Cantons.

In the afternoon about four o'clock we came to Fluellen from where we took a boat-ride on the beautiful Lake of the Four Forest Cantons to Luzerne.

LAKE OF THE FOUR FOREST CANTONS.

This Lake borders on the Cantons of Uri, Unterwalden, Schwytz and Lucerne, in consequence of which it is called *Vierwaldstädter See*, or Lake of the Four Forest Cantons. It branches in different directions, its many bays being named after the principal places located on them. The Lake of Lucerne is its west branch; on the south is the Bay of Alpnach, on the north that of Küssnacht, and Buccbs stretches east and west, while the Bay of Uri forms the south-east end of the lake. It is about twenty-five miles long, its breadth varying. The scenery along the shore is magnificent and romantic. Along its shores, at Küssnacht, at the highest point of the neck of land which divides the Lakes of Zug and Lucerne, is the famous *Hohle Gase*, or Hollow Lane, with Tell's Chapel. It is an unpretentious little edifice with a plain portico and a tiny red spire piercing the foliage of the surrounding trees. Above the door is depicted the death of the tyrant Gessler at the hand of Tell, with a simple inscription, recording the fact.

LUCERNE.

About six o'clock the same evening we landed at Lucerne, and were taken to *Hotel du Cygne*. After supper we went to see the *Löwendenkmal*, a large lion hewed out of the natural rock, his side pierced with a dagger, holding with his right paw the arms of the country, and representing how a few thousand brave Swiss soldiers gave their lives in defense of their little beautiful and romantic country.

Lucerne, the capital of the canton, lies at the north-west of the Lake Lucerne, twenty-five miles south-west of Zürich, ten miles from Mount Rigi, and it has a population of about 16,000. The little town itself is unpretending enough in appearance, but before it stretches the lovely lake in its framework of rocky mountains and grassy hills, combined in a landscape of rich incomparable harmony that the world never tires of admiring its charms. The greatest part of Lucerne (the older portion of the town) lies on the right, bank of the River Reuss, upon a narrow strip of land, between the water and the heights to the north-west. These heights, from the river bank to the gap, through which runs the road to Zürich, are crowned by a long wall, defended by numerous mediæval towers. On the left bank of the river is the lesser town, which extends on one side in the direction of the Lake of Alpnacht, but is bounded lower down the river by the Reuss and precipitous rock, at the foot of, and through which the railway line runs. On the right bank of the lake stands the principal church of the town, the so-called *Hofkirche*, dedicated to St. Leodegar, and surrounded by the quiet dwellings of the clergy and the silent resting places of the dead. Between the older portion of the town and the clerical quarter are several palatial hotels, commanding superb views of the lake and the mountains, and still further out, fringing the right bank, is a whole row of stately hostelries, while numerous comfortable boarding-houses are scattered over the gently sloping hills, which rise tier above tier behind the town. The outline of the lake is crossed by a handsome bridge of modern construction, affording a magnificent view.

The next bridge, the *Kapellenbrücke*, is a very curious structure, built of wood and roofed, and crossing the river in an oblique direction. Above the cross-beams of the roof is a series of quaint old paintings, triangular in form, representing scenes from the history of the town and the confederacy, legends of martyrs, etc., explained by inscriptions and verses still quainter than the pictures. From this bridge a smaller one leads to the ancient octagonal *Wasserthurm*, or Water Tower, rising in the midst of the river; it was intended as a defense against a hostile attack from the lake-side.

Two other bridges follow: the much-frequented *Alte Reussbrücke*, connecting the busiest quarters of the town, and the picturesque *Spreuerbrücke*, which derives its name from the neighboring mills.

Here, at Lucerne, we met Rt. Rev. Bishop W. M. Wigger, D. D., who on account of having taken sick at Rome could not continue the journey with us to Palestine.

The next morning we again took a boat-ride on the Lake of the Four Forest Cantons, up to Vitznau, where we took lunch.

Vitznau, once so solitary, but now the most frequented spot on the banks. This quiet Alpine village has become one of the busiest tourist stations in Europe. Elegant modern buildings have risen among the plain, wooden cottages of the villagers. This little plot of ground suddenly became the scene of a wonderful transformation, for here, where the crack of the coachman's whip had never been heard, and where vehicles of any kind are unknown, a railway terminus was established, and the railroad was seen to boldly scale the heights of the almost inaccessible Mount Rigi—The Vitznau-Rigi Railway.

MOUNT RIGI.

The situation of Vitznau is of unique beauty, especially as seen from the steamboat. The steep and threatening *Vitznauerstock*, one of the shapeliest satellites of the Rigi, the savage gorge descending from the red cliffs near the summit, the *Bürgenstock* across the lake, and above the near headland the *Buechserhorn* and the *Brisen*; these, together with the village and its idyllic surroundings, form a landscape of such surpassing loveliness, that one may well repeat with inward emotion the inscription carved above the portal of the village church: *Soli Deo Gloria!*

We ascended Mount Rigi, which is nearly 9,000 feet high, by a railroad which runs in cog wheels, consisting of one coach and two engines, the one shoving from the rear and the other pulling in front. In ascending there are several stations at which the train stops. The view from its summit is one of the most extensive in the Alps, embracing most of East and North Switzerland and the Jura Mountains. There are numerous hotels along the track, which attract annually as many as 40,000 visitors. This railway, up to *Rigi Kulm*, was completed in 1873. Being up on the top of Mount Rigi, we threw snow-balls. This was the 31st of May. After we had remained on the top for about one hour we again descended by the same way, and took the boat again at Vitznau for Lucerne. After we had eaten supper here our pilgrims took the night express train for Bale and Paris, and here boarded another, which carried them to Havre, where they boarded a Hamburg-American steamer and returned to New York. Rt. Rev. Bishops Wigger, Rademacher, myself and a few more remained at Lucerne, and afterwards traveled into Germany.

The next day, June 1st, early in the morning, I took the train for Maria Einsiedeln.

MARIA EINSIEDELN.

I arrived at Maria Einsiedeln about eleven o'clock in the morning, the distance being forty miles. It is located south-east of Zürich, and has a population of about 8,000. When I came to the Benedictine Abbey I immediately called upon Father Chrysostom Foffa, O. S. B., who was my pastor when I was a little boy, at Fulda, Spencer County, Indiana; he was for many years professor at St. Meinrad's College, in Indiana, and pastor in different large congregations. He also worked with great success for many years among the Indians of Dakota. At present he is professor in the Benedictine Abbey at Einsiedeln, and confessor for the English-speaking people who visit Maria Einsiedeln; he was very much surprised and glad to see me. On this account I was treated royally and immediately taken to the Rt. Rev. Abbot Basilius Oberholzer, who received me very friendly and asked many questions about our pilgrimage to Palestine. After dinner I was kindly shown a room. The Abbot of Einsiedeln stands direct under the Pope.

At about one o'clock P. M. a thousand pilgrims arrived, who were mostly men from the neighboring towns and villages. About seven o'clock in the evening they all came out of the world-renowned church, all having lighted candles in their hands and singing and praying aloud; they marched in procession through the woods to the Statue of St Meinrad. These thousand lights shining through the woods in the dark was a magnificent aspect. When they returned they re-entered the church and remained therein until about nine o'clock. When I came into the church at an early hour the next morning, which was Sunday, it was crowded with people. After about ten o'clock I had the happiness to say Mass in the Holy Chapel called the *Gnaden Kapelle*. There are annually 150,00 or more pilgrims from Switzerland, Germany and Italy, who visit Maria Einsiedeln. The thousandth anniversary of the death of St. Meinrad was celebrated in 1861 with great pomp, and upon which occasion 210,000 pilgrims came to Einsiedeln. Adjoining the village is the famous Benedictine Abbey, founded about the year 900, on the spot where St. Meinrad was murdered.

The present church, built in modern Italian style, and which dates back from 1719, contains a museum and a library of over 30,000 volumes; in one wing of the church is the penitentiary with nineteen confessionals, where confessions in the different languages are heard. I was kindly taken through the monastery. The next morning Father Durwald, one of our pilgrims, also came to Einsiedeln, so in the afternoon he and I left Einsiedeln and returned to Lucerne, where we arrived late in the evening.

The next morning at five o'clock I had my trunk taken to the depot, where I bought my ticket for Basel. Before I left Lucerne my trunk was weighed and I had to pay forty cents; then, instead of giving me a check, they pasted a label on my trunk. This was repeated at every station where I purchased a ticket; sometimes the label was of a yellow, then red, blue, green, white, and, in fact, every conceivable color was brought into effect, so that by the time I arrived at Hamburg my trunk was quite ornamented, and the bruises it got on those donkeys in Egypt and Palestine were entirely invisible.

BASEL.

The City of Basel is situated on the Rhine, forty-five miles north-east of Bern, and is the capital of the canton. It has a population of about 50,000. The city is surrounded by fortifications, which, however, are not very important.

The Canton of Basel is bounded by Alsace, Baden, and the Cantons Aargana, Soloturn and Bern.

The chains of the Jura descend here into the Plains of the Rhine. At Basel I had to pass through the custom-house, but they were not very strict; in fact, the custom-house officials did not have much time, as my train for Strasburg arrived shortly afterward. They asked me what I had in my trunk so I told them I had my clothes and a few little articles which I had purchased on my trip. They believed me, and I was very glad of it. I then bought my ticket and boarded the next train for Strasburg.

STRASBURG.

About two hours afterwards I arrived at Strasburg. Here I had to undergo another examination at the custom-house. Strasburg is the capital of Alsace, Lorraine. It is a city of Germany, and located on the Ill, a tributary of the Rhine; Strasburg is ninety miles south-west of Frankfort, and 250 miles east by south of Paris, and it has a population of about 130,000. It is situated on level ground and is more than seven miles in circumference, and is defended by a wall with bastions and a strong citadel. Opposite Kehl, the Rhine is crossed by a bridge. The Ill flows through the city, and is crossed by several wooden bridges.

Strasburg has several fine squares; its streets are generally narrow, but the principal ones are wide. The houses in Strasburg have steep roofs, but are lofty and well-built.

Its celebrated cathedral, called the *Strasburger Münster*, is one of the finest Gothic churches in Europe. In 1870 it was considerably damaged, but afterwards restored. The famous astronomical clock, made by Isaac Habrecht, in 1570, is one of the greatest works of its kind. I saw the twelve Apostles come out, which takes place twice daily, at twelve o'clock noon and twelve o'clock at night; this is wonderful mechanism. This cathedral is remarkable for its spire, which is an open fretwork of stones, bound together by iron ties, and has a height of 468 feet. In 1439 the tower was completed, but the cathedral was to have a second one which is still unfinished, and therefore mars the effect somewhat. When in 1870 the city was besieged by the Germans, the cathedral was somewhat injured by shells and other projectiles. The cathedral has no pews, but instead of these there are hundreds of chairs piled one above the other, along the wall inside of the nave of the church.

I next went on through Lauterburg to Rheinzabern, near Germersheim, to my reverend uncle; with whom I stopped about two weeks. During this time I went to Karlsruhe where the Grand Duke of Baden resides, and through whose palace I was conducted.

Karlsruhe is the capital of the Grand Duchy of Baden, eighteen miles north-east of Baden-Baden, and has a population of about 45,000. From here I went to Baden-Baden, which is a famous watering place of the Grand Duchy of Baden, situated at the foot of the Black Forest on the Vos. Baden-Baden is eighteen miles south-west of Karlsruhe, and has a population of about 15,000. There are about twenty-five hot springs which flow from the rock at the foot of the castle terrace, the waters of which are conducted in pipes to the different baths throughout the town; the temperature varies from 115° to 154° Fahrenheit. The best season for visitors, whose number annually exceeds 60,000, is in July and August. It has several public baths and numerous good hotels. Its surroundings are beautiful and romantic.

From here I returned to Strasburg, where on Pentecost Sunday I said Mass in the Cathedral.

SPEYER.

In the evening I returned to my uncle and the next day went to Speyer, a town of Bavaria with a population of about 18,000. It is situated six miles north-east of Landau. It has a beautiful cathedral, which is remarkable for its size and antiquity. In the year 1689 the French damaged it, but it has been restored since then with great splendor; it contains the tombs of eight emperors, beneath the church in a basement amongst which is that of Rudolph of Hapsburg. The town became of great importance as the ordinary residence of the emperor of Germany and the seat of the Supreme Court of Appeal. It was laid in ashes May 31, 1689, by the French, but rebuilt in 1699, but it never recovered its former prosperity. It is one of the oldest bishoprics in Germany, and long enjoyed the rights of sovereignty.

From here I went to Germersheim, Pirmasens, Fehrbach, the birthplace of my mother, and to Hohfröschen into the house in which I was born, to Neustadt, Landau, Zweibrücken, and back again to my uncle at Rheinzabern. Then I again went to Speyer, from where I went to

MUNICH.

I left Speyer about ten o'clock A. M., and at about eight o'clock in the evening came to Stuttgart, the capital of the Kingdom of Würtemberg. At eleven o'clock the same night I arrived at Munich.

The next day, when I passed through the streets of the city, I noticed large piles of boards laying in different streets. Presently I met one of the local priests, and inquired of him what was to be done with so many boards. He replied that they would be laid in the streets where the Corpus Christi procession would pass. The next day being Corpus Christi day, I left my hotel early and repaired to the cathedral, which is called "*Frauenkirche*" where I contemplated saying Mass. Even at this early hour the streets were crowded, and as I drew near the cathedral, I found the streets literally blockaded with people. Here a policeman told me that any attempts to enter the church would be fruitless at that time. It required no argument on his part to convince me that he had spoken the truth, and much disappointed, I retreated to a hotel at the nearest corner, and took breakfast. I then asked one of the waiters for permission to remain at one of the windows facing the entrance of the cathedral, in order that I might observe the procession, to which he assented. Here I had a nice opportunity to review this magnificent procession, the largest I had ever seen. The boards which I saw the day previous, were laid along the streets through which the procession passed, from the cathedral on, over their entire route; not lengthwise but across the streets. In front of the cathedral in the open square, several hundred soldiers were mounted on horseback. In the procession over one hundred banners were displayed. Several hundred sisters and students, the majority of the inhabitants (Munich being almost an entirely catholic city), and nearly all the city officers participated; even four or six protestant ministers were obliged to take part, *nolens volens*. The Blessed Sacrament was carried by the Archbishop of

Munich; right behind him, under the baldachim walked the Prince Regent, Luitpold of Bavaria, holding his cap in hand. When the procession returned, I also followed up into the church. After Benediction with the Blessed Sacrament had been given, the archbishop escorted the Prince Regent from the church, after which many Masses were said by those priests who lacked the time or opportunity to do so before.

Munich is the capital of Bavaria on the Isar, on an extensive plain, thirty-three miles south-east of Augsburg, 290 miles south-west of Berlin, and 220 miles west of Vienna. It has about 200,000 inhabitants. Munich is noted for its architectural splendor, its university, and admirable institutions of art. The river Isar is spanned by four bridges; the Isar bridge is the largest, but the Maximilia the finest. Munich has 275 streets. The streets in the old town are irregular but wide. The Ludwig and Maximilian are the most renowned in the new city, which contains the most remarkable public buildings. Among the twenty squares Max-Joseph is the largest; other attractive streets are the Maximilian, Karl and prominade square *"Carolinenplatz', 'Königsplatz'*, and the *'Hofgarten."* Munich has over twenty catholic churches. The Gothic cathedral, has two lofty dome-capped towers. St. Cajetan's contains the tombs of the royal family. The All Saints' Chapel or *"Hofkapelle"* has columns of red Tyrolese marble, with gilded capitals and white bases; above the aisles it is incrusted with colored marble, and the rest is frescoed upon a golden background. In the *"Ludwig' skirche"* are colossal statues of Sts. Peter and Paul, and of the "Last Judgment" which is about sixty feet in height.

The Old Catholic movement has its centre here. Munich has about 6,000 Protestants, and one Jewish synagogue. Its celebrated university named "Ludwig-Maximilian," which was founded in Ingolstadt was removed to Munich in 1826, and attained world-wide celebrity during the reign of Maximilian II. It has several thousand students, over 113 professors, one of whom was the Dr. Ignaz Döllinger, who died at Munich, January 10th, 1890.

The principal royal residences are the Wittelsbach palace, and that of prince Max. I was shown through this one, also that of Prince Luitpold. I also went through the Bavarian National Museum, which is 500 feet long, and ninety-five feet high and contains varied and interesting collections pertaining to Bavarian antiquities. The most conspicuous monument of Munich is the *"Ruhmeshalle"* (hall of fame); Goethe, Schiller, Gluck and many other great men are honored by splendid monuments in the streets and squares of Munich.

The name Munich originates from a settlement of monks (*Mönche*) consequently its name. The king of Bavaria had also a colossal statue called "Bavaria" placed in Munich to perpetuate Bavaria's fame, in the head of which five persons can easily stand. I devoted a small portion of my time to visiting this place. At the season of the year when I was there, a glass of the justly celebrated "*Münchener*" beer, (which is adjudged the finest in the world), is a very tempting beverage, which is here very plentiful. A great resort, for the beer-drinking public in particular, is the "*Löwenbräu Keller.*"

I left Munich for Nuremberg on the morning of June the 21st.

NUREMBERG.

After I had left Munich for about three hours, I came to Ingolstadt, a fortified town of Upper Bavaria, on the left bank of the Danube. At about eleven o'clock the same forenoon I came to Nuremberg (German Nürnberg), in the district of Middle Franconia, on the Ludwig's Canal, ninety-two miles north by west of Munich. It has about 100,000 inhabitants.

The River Pegnitz, on which the city lies, forms three islands that are connected with each other and the city by bridges. By this river the city is divided into two unequal parts; the southern is called the Lorenzer side and the northern the Sebalder side. The general appearance of the city is very antique. Nearly every modern building is built in mediaeval style. It has only two Catholic churches: the one, *Frauenkirche*, is remarkable for its richly ornamented Gothic portal. The city has several elegant public fountains: one on the *Hauptmarkt*, the principal square, is called *der schöne Brunnen*; another is the *Gänsemarkt*, remarkable for the immense number of geese which are here offered for sale; it has also an interesting fountain called *Gänsemännchen*.

Watches were first made here, and were long known as Nuremberg eggs. It is renowned for its industrial activity, especially in lead pencils and looking-glass plates. It is also famous for manufacturing toys, and is one of the principal hop markets of Europe. An active trade with the United States is carried on.

In the afternoon about four o'clock I boarded the train for Würzburg.

WUERZBURG.

I arrived here about nine o'clock in the evening. It is the capital of Lower Franconia, on the right bank of the Main, which is spanned by a large stone bridge, over 600 feet long and of eight arches, with statues of saints. It is 140 miles north-west of Munich, and has a population of about 70,000. The inhabitants are nearly all Catholics. It has fine streets and promenades, although the streets are somewhat irregular. The Episcopal Palace is magnificent. The principal churches are: the cathedral, containing the *Schönborn* chapel and monuments of bishops; the *Marienkapelle* and the *Stifthaug*, built after St. Peter's with an imposing cupola. It has also a renowned and large university, founded in 1403 by Bishop Johann von Eglofstein.

Würzburg lies low. Here I heard the nicest ringing of bells I had ever heard. During my stay in Bavaria the church bells had to ring from twelve to one o'clock every day for a month, on account of the death of the mother of the king. Würzburg is known for the nice ringing of its bells. The King of Bavaria has here a magnificent palace, through which I was taken. It was built by the bishops of Würzburg. In this place there one hall which is 600 feet long; one room is specially noteworthy; it is called *das Spiegelzimmer*, and is said to have cost two millions of German *Gulden*. Near the city, on St. Nicolaus Mountain, is a splendid pilgrimage church called *Kapelle*, which I also went to see. Going up is the Way of the Cross—fourteen massive chapels built of stone. Around the city a great deal of wine and fruit is raised. Würzberg dates from the sixth century. St. Kilian is said to have preached the gospel here as early as the year 688.

About two o'clock P. M. the next day I took the train for Frankfort-on-the-Main.

FRANKFORT-ON-THE-MAIN.

I arrived here at seven o'clock in the evening of June 22d. This city is in the Prussian province of Hesse-Nassau, situated in a fertile valley on the right bank of the River Main, twenty miles above its confluence with the River Rhine. It is 255 miles south-west of Berlin, and has a population of about 150,000. The finest street is the Zeil, which was afterwards united with the *Neue Kräme*. Among the most remarkable public squares are the *Rossmarkt*, which has a monument in honor of the art of printing, the Goethe Square with a grand statue of the poet, by Schwanthaler, who was born here, and Schiller Square, and his statue, and the "*Römerberg*." On this latter is the "*Römer*" or council house in which the German emperors were elected, and in its "*Kaisersaal*" were entertained. On its walls hang the portraits of the emperors. The principal business streets, are the "*Fahrgasse*" and "*Schnurgasse*;" among the fine streets are the avenues near the gates of the city and the "*Schöne Aussicht*."

Frankfort is surrounded by promenades and they are indeed among the finest pleasure grounds in Europe. It has one of the best theatres in Germany. The chief local manufactures are carpets, table covers, jewelry, playing cards, oil cloth and tobacco. It has also a very extensive and interesting Zoological garden which I visited.

The next day at one o'clock I boarded the train for Mentz.

MENTZ (GER. MAINZ.)

Here I arrived at about two o'clock in the afternoon. Mentz is a fortified city of Germany and the capital of Rhenish Hesse, on the left bank of the Rhine, nearly opposite its junction with the Main. It is twenty miles southwest of Frankfort, and has a population of about 70,000. It is connected with the village of Castel on the opposite bank of the Rhine, by a pontoon bridge, 1,700 feet long. It has also a very expensive railroad bridge finished in 1864, which connects it with the opposite side of the Main. The town, looked at from the river, has the appearance of an amphitheatre. Its houses are lofty, but its streets confined and narrow. The city has eleven churches.

Mentz is one of the chief centres of the Catholic Societies of Germany. It has also a very elegant Cathedral. The trade of Mentz up and down the Rhine and the Main is immense. Already during the time of St. Boniface it became the seat of an archbishop.

The next morning at ten o'clock I took the boat "Adolph" on the Rhine for Cologne.

THE RHINE.

One of Europe's principal rivers is the Rhine, which has its source in the Swiss Canton of Grisons, and flows into the North Sea in Holland. It generally flows north-west, and is about 800 miles long. It is divided into three parts, the Upper, Middle, and Lower: the first part lies within and along the line of Switzerland; the second, between Basel and Cologne: and the third, between Cologne and the sea. It is joined at Dissentes by the Middle Rhine from the right; it then flows generally in an east by north direction about thirty-six miles to Reichenau, where it is about 180 feet wide, and navigable for boats. It afterwards flows in a northerly direction to the Lake of Constance, past Constance. It takes a westerly direction for some distance, until it enters the Falls of Schaffhausen. From the Lake of Constance to Basel it reaches its boundary line between Baden and Switzerland. At Basel, where the Middle Rhine begins, it changes its course in a northerly direction; it flows for about 200 miles to Mentz, along a valley, thirty to fifty miles wide, extending on the east between the Black Forest, and on the west between the Hardt Mountains, which form the boundary of Baden and Alsace, and Baden and Rhenish Bavaria. Between Strasburg and Metz the Rhine is navigable for boats of about 100 tons burden. Between Mentz and Cologne, which is a distance of 120 miles, the course of the river is west; afterwards north-west. Near Coblentz it enters the Prussian Rhine Province. This part of the river runs between two mountain regions; here the river is so narrow as to hardly allow passage for a boat.

The wine raised in the extensive vineyards in this neighborhood, is known as Rhenish wine. From Cologne to its mouth, a distance of 300 miles, the

Lower Rhine flows through a low country and near its east bank the hills of Sauerland between Cologne and Düsseldorf. From Wesel to the frontiers of Holland its course is north-west. After having entered Holland, the Rhine branches off into two arms; the one to the north retains its name, the other to the south, is called Waal.

COLOGNE.

At Mentz, as stated above, I took the boat down to Cologne, which is the finest passage on the entire Rhine. As soon as we came in sight of the beautiful city of Cologne all the passengers left their seats, and comments on the world-renowned Dome of Cologne, were pleasantly indulged in. This Dome majestically overlooks the entire city, and can be seen for miles and miles before reaching the city. We arrived at Cologne in the evening about six o'clock.

Cologne is the capital of the Rhenish province and is situated on the left bank of the Rhine; it is thirty-eight miles north-east of Aix-la-Chapelle. It numbers over 200,000 inhabitants, who are mostly Catholics. Opposite Cologne is the city of Deutz, which is connected with Cologne by a pontoon bridge, and also an iron railway bridge 1,352 feet long. Cologne forms a semi-circle resting upon the Rhein and is protected by forts. Its streets are mostly narrow.

The Cathedral.

The pride of Cologne is that remarkable structure, the Cathedral. This is the largest specimen of Gothic architecture in the world; it is 511 feet long, and 231 feet wide; its towers are also 511 feet high. This cathedral was begun about the middle of the thirteenth century. The first stone of the transept was laid in 1842 by Frederick William IV. Outside it has a double range of flying buttresses and intervening piers; it is a perfect forest of pinnacles. The government contributed a large sum towards its completion; money was also raised by private subscription, and by the *"Dombauverein"* which had branches throughout Europe. In this cathedral is also a beautiful monument dedicated to the three Holy Kings, of whom some bones are here deposited. During my stay at Cologne I said Mass in the Dome.

In 1848 its nave, aisles and transept were consecrated. The other most important churches of Cologne are: St. Gereon, St. Peter and St. Ursula; that of the Apostles is the finest of those latter named.

In 1794 Cologne fell into the hands of the French, but in 1814 it was restored to Prussia. Cologne is connected by railroads, with all the principal cities of the continent.

I left Cologne on June 26, taking the six o'clock A. M., train for Hamburg.

HAMBURG.

After having stopped at Bremen three hours, I reached Hamburg at about eight o'clock P. M.

Hamburg is on the north bank of the Elbe, at the mouth of the Alster, sixty miles north-east of Bremen. The Alster, a tributary of the Elbe, flows through the city; there are also numerous canals that interesect the city. A magnificent bridge, completed in 1872, crosses the Elbe, and sixty other bridges span the rivers and canals. Hamburg is in connection, by railway, with the leading German cities, and by steamship with the principal ports of Europe, and with New York, New Orleans, Havana and Brazil. It has 400,000 inhabitants. There are only two Catholic churches. Hamburg is one of the largest harbors of Europe, it ranking next to Liverpool.

Sunday morning at nine o'clock, June 30th, I left Hamburg. At the dock I met, to my great surprise, Mr. John Hoebing, one of our pilgrims, who also was destined for New York. In a small boat we were taken out about two hours and put on the steamer "Moravia," of the Hamburg-American Company. At twelve o'clock the steamer started. Tuesday at four o'clock A. M. we came near Havre; here our steamer had to stop on account of the tide until twelve o'clock, when it had risen somewhat; a small boat pulled our steamer into Havre. All afternoon they loaded freight and coal, so we stopped off and went into the city. At twelve o'clock at night the steamer started again and we had a good voyage on the Atlantic. I felt much better the whole time than I did, while writing this history, although some of the passengers that were on the ocean for the first time complained of being sea-sick. Saturday, July 13th, we came to New York, and it being late in the evening we did not land until the next morning.

This, now, my dear reader, ends the history of the First American Catholic Pilgrimage to Palestine and my six months' trip. I here also can say with the Psalmist:

"*Non nobis, Domine, non nobis, sed nomini tuo gloriam.*"

www.ingramcontent.com/pod-product-compliance
Lightning Source LLC
Chambersburg PA
CBHW020425010526
44118CB00010B/424